Pardon and Peace

Pardon and Peace
A reflection on the making of peace in Ireland

NICHOLAS FRAYLING

First published in Great Britain 1996
The Society for Promoting Christian Knowledge
Holy Trinity Church
Marylebone Road
London NW1 4DU

Second impression, with corrections, 1996

British Library Cataloguing in Publication Data

A catalogue record of this book is available from the British Library

ISBN 0-281-04933-5

Typeset by David Gregson Associates, Beccles, Suffolk
Printed and bound in Great Britain by
The Cromwell Press, Melksham, Wiltshire

For
David, Derek and John
who have tried so hard
to demonstrate that
there is no fear in love

Contents

Foreword

by the Church Leaders of Merseyside

Canon Nicholas Frayling is an Englishman who has strong links, both personal and pastoral, with Ireland. His ancestry is partly Irish, and as Rector of Liverpool he is deeply conscious of the Irish component in the city's history and its present life.

We have seen and admired his deep commitment to the City Centre Ecumenical Team here in Liverpool. He plays an important role in ridding this city of sectarian suspicion and rivalry and building partnership and trust.

Though he disclaims any specialist knowledge of Irish history, he understands it better than the vast majority of British people. His knowledge has not come solely from books, but from listening long and hard to Irish people telling their stories, stories often laced with pain and suffering.

Much of that pain and suffering stems from the treatment which Britain has meted out to the Irish people over the centuries. Canon Frayling does not deny the need for economic and political change in Ireland. Yet, he argues, that alone is not enough. The deeper need is to change hearts and minds, to dispel fear and suspicion, hatred and guilt, the poisonous legacy of a complicated past.

How is that to be done? By facing the truth about our history, our wrongdoing; repenting of it, and so enabling a 'healing of the memories', and a new beginning. The Irish parties to the present conflict have, of course, their own agenda for penitence. Canon Frayling, however, writes as an Englishman and addresses his own fellow-citizens and fellow-Christians. If we are serious about pardon and peace, let it begin with us.

He does not pretend that the way of penitence, forgiveness and reconciliation is easy. It is certain to be costly, as South Africa has found. He recognizes that there are enormous fears to overcome.

Yet fear is, proverbially, a bad counsellor. One of the strengths of the author's approach is that he has genuinely striven to listen to Irish people, of all shades of political and religious conviction. In what he calls the 'verbatimness' of the narrative, we hear the living voice of people, across a wide spectrum, who are deeply involved in the tragedy of Ireland.

He acknowledges that religion has been and is part of the Irish problem. Yet that is not the whole story. Christians have often been challenged to show that their Faith has anything distinctive to contribute to the healing of the wounds of Ireland. Here, rooted in faith in the Lord who cries from the cross, 'Father, forgive them', is one Christian priest's answer. We are confident that it deserves widespread consideration and support.

John A. Newton, Ex-President, Churches Together in England
David Sheppard, Bishop of Liverpool
Derek Worlock, Archbishop of Liverpool

Preface

English people who say they love Ireland and Irish people are often perceived as patronizing or insincere. Given the eight or more centuries of conflict between our two islands, such a reaction is not surprising. That I have encountered it very rarely in the past twenty years is a cause of great astonishment to me, for I have to declare that I do love Ireland.

Apart from occasional childhood holidays, I have been a regular visitor to the Republic and, though less frequently, to the North, since the mid-1970s. I can truthfully say that some of the most important and precious friendships of my life have been forged with Irish and Northern Irish people. This, together with the natural beauty of the country, has made it all the more difficult to comprehend the agony within that island, which is so casually dismissed in Britain as 'the troubles' or 'the Irish problem'.

Ireland, the North and the Republic, as I was often reminded, has been bedevilled by people from across the water who think they know what is best for its peoples. Why, then, have I felt led to write this book? First, because although a huge number of books have been written about Britain and Ireland, and the problems in the North, I have found most to be daunting for the nonspecialist reader, like me! Second, I want to share a very personal journey of discovery.

This book tells the story of my love of Ireland and how it came about. It describes how I became uneasy, and then ashamed, as I read, listened and tried to learn about the way in which the nation to which I belong has dealt with Ireland and its peoples over many centuries. The record is not a happy one. Some of these painful issues are being addressed in what has come to be known as 'the peace process', but the roots of the conflict within the island of Ireland go back centuries, and it may be that something more than politics is required to bring about true and lasting reconciliation and the healing of memories. That is the theme of this book.

I have said that this is a very personal record. I make no apology for that: indeed, my bishop wrote, 'Your personal story is your justification for entering this crowded field.' I am a priest in the Church of England, so naturally there are Christian thoughts and insights within the story. I believe, however, that what I have to say may also be of interest to those who do not share my faith.

Many people have told me that they are almost completely ignorant of the history of Ireland, so I have included, in Appendix 1, a short background history, for those who wish to refer to it. Indeed, I should like to suggest that readers might begin there: it provides a useful background to the rest of the book.

Much has happened in Northern Ireland since I completed the first draft, and it would be a rash person who predicted the outcome of the peace process, even in the short term. Many of the conversations I had (some of which are reproduced in chapters eight and nine) indicate a level of fear and uncertainty which is hard for people in Britain to comprehend. They have left me pondering the distinction between hope and optimism.

It is my real hope that my own journey may help others, especially in Britain, to understand more about the island of Ireland, its peoples and their concerns, and perhaps be led to pray and work for reconciliation. (A second appendix provides a list of organizations committed to this work.) Better still, they may wish to make their own journey of discovery.

Acknowledgements

Many people have helped me to write this book. Very few of them are named in the text, for reasons which will become apparent to the reader. I am deeply grateful to all of them, especially to those who have opened their homes to me with the hospitality for which the people of Ireland are justly famous, or who have been generous with their time. Many have been startlingly honest. I hope I have betrayed no one's trust.

I am grateful to the Church of Ireland Theological College in Dublin, which provided me with a base during a period of sabbatical study leave in 1994 – in particular, the principal, staff and students, who were extremely kind, and showed a keen interest in my activities.

My ordained colleagues at Liverpool Parish Church, Dennis Capes, John Williams and Steve Williams, have taken on much extra work, and been unstinting in their encouragement, as have the members of the congregation, who have borne what one called my Irish obsession with patience and understanding. My fellow-members in the Liverpool City Centre Ecumenical Team have shared much of this book. I cannot begin to say how much their fellowship in the gospel means to me. Certainly we have begun to learn, together, where friendship, prayer and trust might lead.

I should like to express special thanks to my long-suffering secretary, Maureen Trapnell, who has cheerfully taken on much extra work while I have been writing this book, and helped enormously in its production; to James Muirhead, who, with quiet efficiency, helped me deal with hundreds of letters and other papers, especially while I was travelling; and to Annie and James Butterworth, who read the first draft of this book, and made many uncomfortable but always perceptive suggestions. That is true also of Rachel Boulding at SPCK, to whom I express particular gratitude for her patience and skill.

Finally, I am indebted to the three Merseyside Church Leaders, the Revd Dr John Newton and the Most Revd Derek Worlock, both of whom have recently announced their retirements, and my own bishop, the Rt Revd David Sheppard. Each of them has constantly encouraged me. My dedication of this book to them says it all.

Nicholas Frayling
Dublin, Belfast, Sées, Liverpool
May 1994–September 1995

Note to Second Edition

An early reprint has enabled me to make some minor corrections to the text. It also gives me an opportunity to record, with great regret, the death of Archbishop Derek Worlock, shortly before the book was published. I shall always remember his encouragement and a long conversation we had about Ireland, a couple of weeks before he died.

I have received a great many letters from people who care about Ireland, especially in the light of the breakdown of the IRA ceasefire and events in Northern Ireland during the 'marching season' of 1996. One correspondent described this book as 'little better than a recruiting pamphlet for Sinn Fein', another as 'a predictable eulogy by an Englishman of the Ulster Protestants'.

I continue to believe (and, of course, to hope and pray) that *Pardon and Peace* offers a way forward.

Nicholas Frayling
Liverpool, September 1996

1 *The journey begins*

When I was a theological student, I spent several holidays in the Irish Republic. On one occasion, three of us were given the red-carpet treatment in a bed and breakfast establishment, a farm in the midlands. While cleaning one of the rooms in the morning, the landlady discovered a Bible and a Prayer Book. 'You did say you were training to be priests? Now I find you're Protestants. You should have told me. I'd still have taken you, but at least I'd have known.'

We tried to make amends by encouraging conversation about Scripture and Catholicism; we even admired the picture of the Sacred Heart on the living-room wall; but something had changed.

There was an amusing but uncomfortable sequel. Some six years later, in the bar of a pub in my parish in south London, I was recounting this story to some Irish friends; I am ashamed to say it lost nothing in the telling. One of my audience was an enormous labourer called Sean, whom I had first met years before in my professional capacity as a welfare officer at Pentonville Prison. Sean broke into my account: 'That would have been Mrs Joyce. She was my auntie, God rest her. I'm surprised you of all people should speak ill of the dead.'

It is, as they say, a small world, but that sort of 'coincidence' has been a constant feature of my Irish journey. In 1975 my car, an ancient Ford Popular without a jack, suffered a puncture in the middle of Connemara. It was past ten o'clock at night and pouring with rain. I struck out for the lights of a cottage. The door was opened by a tall young man who took one look at me and said, 'You'll take a drink, Father Nick.' It was a statement, not a question. Colm was a gravedigger at Streatham Cemetery, visiting his mother in the west of Ireland. I took him at his word, several times over, and spent the night on the floor, having declined to share the only bedroom with the two of them.

The parish of which I was Vicar from 1974 to 1983 was in Tooting, south west London. It is an area with a large immigrant Irish population. Although there was little formal ecumenical contact with the two enormous local Roman Catholic parishes, I got to know a great many Irish people, and was a welcome and regular guest in more than a dozen homes. Most people were reticent on the subject of Britain and Ireland, at least in my presence, but I remember a Sunday dinner with a builder and his family. Pat broke a glass as he thumped the table, with the words, 'There'll be no peace in Ireland, I tell you, until there is justice.' His wife sought to cool the situation by saying, 'Come on, dear, the Vicar won't want to know about that sort of thing.' But he did.

In the summer of 1976 I spent a further holiday in Connemara, this time in a small hotel in a fishing village. Sitting in the bar one evening – it was the 21st of July – my attention was caught by the BBC television news, chiefly because I happened to know the newsreader. Kenneth Kendall announced that the British Ambassador to Ireland, Christopher Ewart-Biggs, had been killed when a landmine exploded underneath his car in Dublin, and that the Secretary of State for Northern Ireland, Merlyn Rees, had been expected to travel in the same car. The bar went silent. I was the only English person present. I decided it would be prudent to leave.

'Where would you be thinking of going, sir?' The man on the next stool at the bar put a hand on my arm. I said I thought I might take a walk. 'Better not,' he said. 'You'll stay and have a drink.' Guinness was produced, and the man continued, 'I want you to know one thing. None of us have any time for your government, but that (pointing at the television) is something else. God help that poor man's family.'

There followed some four hours of conversation, in which every single man took part – there were no women present. We talked about what I had always dismissed as 'the Irish problem'; or rather, they talked and I listened. Nobody left. Nobody seemed to expect the bar to close. At about two o'clock in the morning, I was rash enough to say that I played the piano (though by that time I had almost to be shown the way to the instrument) and a book of Irish rebel songs was produced. Several choruses later, I asked rather weakly when, or if, the bar was going to close. The answer came immediately, 'When we wake the Sergeant in the corner.' Eventually someone prodded the leg of that gentleman, who stretched himself, gazed around, and said, with all the dignity of his rank, 'Time now, boys.' Dawn was breaking over the hills.

That evening, tragic, bizarre, unexpected and so informative, was for me a rite of passage. Although the version of history with which I was presented was unashamedly partisan, I was astonished by the passion and the knowledge of those men, and their deep sense of personal identification with the history of their land. I could not imagine such a conversation, at least one which involved everybody, in an English pub.

Years later I recounted the story of that evening to the Ambassador's widow, Lady Jane Ewart-Biggs, whom I had invited to give an address in Liverpool Parish Church. She was delighted to learn of my interest in Ireland, and how it came about; she told me it would have made Christopher very happy.

I began to read about the history of Britain and Ireland. Nearly all the books I found presented the story from a British (and usually an English) point of view. This began to raise many questions in my mind. However, the demands of a very large parish made it impossible for me to pursue them for the time being.

NATIONAL SORROW

In August 1979, along with most people in Britain and, as I later discovered, in Ireland, I was horrified by the murder at Mullaghmore, in the north west of the Republic, of Earl Mountbatten, along with his grandson, a young boatman and Lady Brabourne. This terrible event was followed within hours by the deaths in an ambush of eighteen British soldiers at Warrenpoint in County Down, Northern Ireland.

There was something uniquely poignant about Mountbatten's death. Apart from the fact that he was the Queen's cousin, he was such a widely admired figure in Britain, and almost eighty years of age. For more than thirty years he had spent the month of August at his home in Mullaghmore. He did not have special protection, since everybody knew him, and he never believed he would be in any danger.

It happened that I was in the west of Scotland on the day of his funeral, which I heard on my car radio, looking out across the Sound of Sleat towards the Hebrides and Ireland. In a moment of heightened awareness and deep emotion which I have never been able to explain in rational terms, I realized that there would never be peace in Ireland until there was an expression of sorrow for all the hurt and injustice which had been done to the Irish people. I was equally certain that the primary obligation for that sorrow, and its public expression, lay first and foremost with Britain. As I listened to the funeral service – the stately liturgy so typical of the Church of England at times of national sorrow – such ideas seemed wildly inappropriate, even treacherous. I therefore decided to tell no one, but to write down my thoughts and feelings, and see whether an opportunity might later present itself to express them in public.

TWO CATHEDRALS AND A FOOTBALL MATCH

In 1983, to my great surprise, I was invited to become Canon Precentor of Liverpool Cathedral, a post which gave me particular responsibility for ordering the worship in that great building, which dominates the skyline from all over Merseyside. At the same time, I was able to renew existing friendships in the city, and to discover the rich diversity of cultures which make up the 'Scouse' community.

The year 1985 was an especially significant one for the churches in the Merseyside region. On Whit Sunday – the Feast of Pentecost – a Covenant for Unity was signed by the leaders of all the principal Christian denominations. It was my task to produce the first draft of the service, which was to be held in both Liverpool's cathedrals, incorporating a procession along Hope Street from one to the other.

It was a wonderful day. A crowd of 5,000 crammed into the Roman Catholic Metropolitan Cathedral of Christ the King, more affectionately known in Liverpool as Paddy's Wigwam, for the first half of the service. All then moved to the Anglican

Cathedral Church of Christ for the signing of the Deed of Covenant, which pledged each denomination to work ceaselessly for the unity of all Christians, in accordance with Christ's will.

A small group of extreme Protestants screamed abuse as the procession, led by the Church leaders, walked past them, but this did little to dispel the deep sense of joy which was felt by the participants. It was sad that the protesters, numbering no more than thirty, seized the headlines in the media.

For me, the happiness of the day was somewhat marred by the pressing attentions of a very large lady – she was Irish, I regret to say – who was convinced that I was the Archbishop of Canterbury. She flung her arms around me as I processed up the nave of our Cathedral, and, giving me a very beery kiss, said, 'God, I love you, Dr Runcie!' As a consequence, I missed the signing of the Covenant. I was trying, with the rather ineffective assistance of two nuns, to keep my admirer (or rather, Archbishop Runcie's) at arm's length.

Ecumenism in Liverpool is an extraordinary phenomenon. Liverpool is a city in which Orange and Green tensions have in the past rivalled those of Northern Ireland, and where sectarian divisions have been particularly vicious. Within living memory, for example, there were parts of the city into which Archbishop Heenan never ventured, for fear that his car would be stoned by Orangemen, and large areas would be brought to a standstill by the parades which marked St Patrick's Day and the anniversary of the Battle of the Boyne.

Out of this bitter context has emerged what has become known as 'The Mersey Miracle'. The public ecumenism of Archbishop Derek Worlock and Bishop David Sheppard has inspired many people, well beyond Merseyside. Their joint activities were well described in their book *Better Together*,[1] and recently *With Hope in Our Hearts*,[2] and have been developing over twenty years. Described affectionately as Fish and Chips ('always together and never out of the paper') their partnership has been enriched by the inclusion of Free Church moderators, of whom the latest has been the distinguished Methodist, Dr John Newton.

In the same year, I was involved in preparing a very different act of worship. On 29 May 1985 in Heysel, in Belgium, a football match was held between Liverpool and Juventus of Turin. Fighting broke out on the terraces between the rival supporters. Twenty-seven people died. Whoever was responsible – and poor ticket-control, a dilapidated stadium and inefficient policing were all found to have played a part – the fact remained that the Liverpool supporters were widely blamed, and the city went into a state of shock. A French television crew caught me unawares outside the cathedral and asked me, in front of camera, what it felt like to be a priest in such a *ville barbare* (barbaric city), and whether I thought religion could have any effect on such *bandits* (thugs).

The Roman Catholic authorities moved very quickly, and celebrated a Requiem Mass a day or two after the tragedy. This was widely appreciated, and gave the opportunity for an outpouring of grief. It was decided that a further service should be held, a week later, in the Anglican Cathedral. This presented certain difficulties for us. What should be its theme or tone? The feeling was growing that the Liverpool fans had been unjustly maligned in the media, and there were those who felt that the service itself was a mistake. When it became known that members of the Royal Family, the Prime Minister and other political leaders were to be present, it was clear that security would have to be very tight and seating would be limited. Plans were made to relay the service on giant screens outside. It would also be broadcast live on television.

All these considerations meant that the event would have to be very different from the spontaneous expression of grief and prayer in the Roman Catholic Cathedral. It had, in effect, become a national event. We decided that the service should be, in name and, as far as possible in reality, 'A Service of Sorrow and Penitence, in Hope of Reconciliation'. The centrepiece was the presentation, by the Lord Lieutenant of Merseyside, of Tokens of Sorrow to the Italian and Belgian people. As the Cathedral choir sang quietly, silver salvers, engraved with messages of sorrow from the people of Liverpool, were received by the ambassadors of the two countries. At the conclusion of the service, a huge Candle of Remembrance was lit by a little child, and a Book of Condolence was inaugurated by the distinguished visitors. This book was signed by several thousand people in the following two weeks, before being presented to the City of Turin.

After the service, the Belgian ambassador asked, 'Why have you done this? This terrible thing was not Liverpool's fault.' I remember replying that somebody has always to make the first move.

The Italian ambassador said he had been deeply moved, and that he was amazed by the generosity of the gesture, which he would make sure was well-reported in Italy. It would, he felt, be extremely helpful in bringing about better relations between our two cities. Civic and church leaders subsequently went to Turin on a mission of reconciliation which was widely reported in the Italian media.

The Heysel service made a deep impression on me at the time. It was to have a profound effect on my life and ministry for many years to come.

2 *A model of togetherness*

The significance of the Heysel service and its theme was not fully apparent to me until I witnessed the powerful effect of the event on those who were present. I began to understand the healing possibilities of corporate repentance, and Britain and Ireland again came to mind. I did not at that time know that others, notably Bishop John Baker, had been urging repentance by Britain towards Ireland, or indeed that similar views had been expressed a century earlier by Cardinal Henry Manning.

In 1987 I received a wholly unexpected letter from Sir William Gladstone, asking if I would like to be considered for the post of Rector of Liverpool. Many parishes in the Church of England are still in the hands of private patrons, who are able, with the consent of the bishop of the diocese, to 'present' clergy as rectors or vicars. It is a system of which many bishops disapprove! It must be said that, on the face of it, it is a very odd way to go about such matters. However, if the patron is a person of Christian commitment who is prepared to study the needs of the parish, the system can work very well, and lead to unlikely and imaginative appointments. It is hardly for me to comment in the case of Liverpool Parish Church.

William Ewart Gladstone, the great Victorian Prime Minister, became occupied, if not obsessed, with Ireland and the issue of Home Rule. Indeed, he wrecked his political career and, some believe, the Liberal Party as well, by his single-mindedness on the subject. It became, for him, a matter of conscience. Gladstone was a 'High Anglican', and was dismayed when Disraeli, a convert to Christianity, was able as Prime Minister to appoint a markedly evangelical bishop, J. C. Ryle, for the newly-created Diocese of Liverpool. Gladstone acquired the rights of patronage of two or three parishes in the new diocese, of which the Parish of Our Lady and St Nicholas, on the waterfront, would ensure an Anglo-Catholic presence in the heart of the city.

I was summoned to Hawarden Castle in North Wales, where Gladstone's study remains just as it was when he died in 1898, to be interviewed by his great-grandson. The interview was a searching one, but I was eventually offered the post, and decided to accept.

ON THE WATERFRONT

The Parish of Liverpool is a curious one. In the past two centuries it has absorbed some twenty-seven other parishes, with the result that it now comprises most of the city centre, and the area of Vauxhall to the north. It was to Vauxhall, by the docks, that thousands of the most destitute of the Irish emigrants came to settle in the years following the great famine of the 1840s. Lacking the resources and the physical strength to make the journey to America or Australia, or even to other British cities, they remained where they landed. Many died. To this day, the population of that part of the parish remains about ninety-five per cent Roman Catholic. Liverpool Parish Church, I discovered, had a covenant partnership with the local Roman Catholic parish of St Mary's, Highfield Street, the earliest Catholic parish in the city. As Rector, I was also to be a member of the Liverpool City Centre Ecumenical Team of clergy.

Over the past seven years, I have learned, for the first time in an ordained ministry of over twenty years, the pleasure, the pain and the potential of ecumenical work, and its great importance. In Liverpool, the team is in effect a confederation of priests and ministers belonging to denominations which are affiliated to the Merseyside and Region Churches Ecumenical Assembly. At the present time, this includes clergy of the Anglican, Methodist, Roman Catholic and United Reformed Churches.

The team offers chaplaincy to companies and institutions within the city centre. This is carried out by means of what we call 'representative ministry'. This means that individual clergy visit on behalf of the whole team or, as we prefer to think, the whole Church of God. There are occasions when it is right to refer particular people to a minister of their own denomination, but the whole basis of the approach is our belief that mission and pastoral care are best carried out ecumenically, and that we have gone beyond the point where it is necessary for people to visit in pairs, or groups, of different traditions.

Such a way of working raises sharp questions and theological issues, which we try not to duck. For all the difficulties which arise, it can provide a powerful witness, and not least in a city with Liverpool's history of sectarian division. I recall a particularly significant occasion. A senior police officer's son died in tragic circumstances, and the bereaved family wanted the headquarters chaplain to conduct the funeral. The family was Protestant, the chaplain Roman Catholic. Nonetheless, he conducted the funeral in the family's Anglican parish church, with the assistance of the parish deacon, a woman. That service made a very deep impression on all who were present. A bishop in the Church of Ireland later told me such an occurrence was not only unthinkable in Ireland, but also highly undesirable.

FRIENDSHIP, MEETING AND PRAYER

We in the ecumenical team have come to regard such a method of working almost as the norm, and have been delighted to welcome visitors from other parts of Britain, from Scandinavia, Holland and Germany, who have come to see how we work. We are eager to share our ecumenical experience as widely as possible.

It would be misleading to give the impression that this process has been easy. The key ingredient is trust between team members, and that takes a long time to build. It depends upon personal friendship and regular meeting, and it depends crucially upon a discipline of prayer. But there is also pain. Inevitably we are brought face to face with the practices of each others' churches, and sometimes their restrictions. Thus, for example, non-Roman Catholics are not permitted to share fully in the Mass, and nor are Catholics themselves permited to share fully in the Communion services of other denominations. We are also brought face to face with each others' doctrinal and, no less significantly, cultural formation. We try to give time to working out what really is fundamental to faith and practice, and what is merely of secondary importance. It is worth the effort.

At a time when all the Christian denominations are in decline, ecumenical partnership is all the more important, 'that the world may believe' (John 17.21). For me, these years have been a powerful learning experience. The most significant lesson has been that ecumenism is about truth. It has nothing to do with uniformity, and it involves no compromise of integrity. Rather, it has led us to an appreciation of the richness and diversity which every tradition of the Christian Church has to contribute to the whole. What is more, ecumenical co-operation enables clergy and their congregations to observe and experience other forms of worship, with the result that walls of inherited prejudice are broken down.

I think of an elderly Methodist woman who said, after attending a Roman Catholic Mass in the Week of Prayer for Unity, 'That service was so much more biblical than ours. I was brought up to believe it was blasphemous. It's all very confusing.' Or a Roman Catholic businessman, after a Free Church service in which extempore prayer had been offered: 'I have felt closer to God today, in a more personal way, than in any service I have ever attended. What have we all been missing?'

The ecumenical experience which we share has made it all the more important for me to discover Liverpool's sectarian past, and to investigate such tensions elsewhere, especially in Northern Ireland. As a result of the sharing of duties within the clergy team at Liverpool Parish Church, I have been enabled to find time to think about Ireland, in the heart of a city which has been shaped by Ireland and Irish people from its foundation. When King John, in 1210, needed a deep-water port from which to embark an army to Ireland, and chose the Mersey estuary, he effectively established the Port of Liverpool. The present Parish Church of Our Lady and St Nicholas is the successor of the earliest seafarers' chapel, dedicated to 'St Mary del Key' (St Mary of the Quay) in 1257.

ANOTHER CATHEDRAL AND AN INVITATION

In May 1992 I was invited by the Provost and Chapter to preach a sermon in Southwark Cathedral in south London, the cathedral in which I had been ordained twenty-one years previously. There was nothing especially significant about the day, but I regarded it as a great honour, and I determined to use that influential London pulpit to express, for the first time, my views about Britain and Ireland.

In my sermon, I described the Heysel service in Liverpool, and went on to suggest certain useful parallels, in particular the conviction that there could be no lasting reconciliation between Britain and the Irish people without sorrow and penitence. I pointed out the disastrous record of English involvement in the affairs of Ireland throughout much of its history. I went on to outline particular 'landmarks' in that history, and tried to show how my own city of Liverpool has been shaped, politically, commercially, socially and religiously by Ireland. I suggested that we need to learn our history if we are ever to be able to set it aside. Evil things have been said and done over several centuries, and at some point that reality has to be faced, instead of trying, by military and other means, to deal only with consequences. History, after all, shapes our attitudes, and that is especially true of our attitude towards Ireland and the Irish people.

I tried to spell out the theological proposition that, without acknowledgement of responsibility, or at least partial responsibility, there could be no real penitence, and without that, no possibility of reconciliation. In this connection the Heysel event and its aftermath, though apparently very far from the complexities of Britain and Ireland, did have something to teach us.

Bishop John Baker had written, in 1984:

> We have to ask what it is that makes differences, which in other societies can be tolerated, intolerable in Northern Ireland, even in contemplation. For what we have is the sight of one section of the people saying to the rest, 'We could never live in a country where you were in the majority.' Now that is deeply hurtful: it is an insult.[1]

The only way to begin to overcome that 'fatal legacy' was by sorrow and penitence, in hope of reconciliation. That, after all, is the Church's formula. It once united a hurt city, and it made possible a new beginning. Some will object that such a notion is spiritual naiveté, which has no place in the harsh world of politics, but it is a fundamental Christian insight that, when people become seized with fear and hatred, the Spirit of Christ can liberate.

I concluded my sermon at Southwark by suggesting that it was for that very reason that we need have no fear to address the bitter legacy of Irish history, and to acknowledge shame for past and present evils, in hope of reconciliation. If reconciliation is God's way, then it must be possible to achieve it, and by his methods.

By one of those coincidences that seem to run through this narrative, a retired American Senator happened to be in the congregation that morning. He told me that his grandparents had emigrated from Ireland through the Port of Liverpool. He went on to say, 'You have said what I have always thought, deep down, but never uttered, for fear of discourtesy to our British friends and allies.'

I gave him a copy of the sermon. I never heard again from him, directly. However, early in 1993 I received an invitation to take part in an international conference to be held in Richmond, Virginia, on the theme 'Healing the Heart of America – an honest conversation on Race, Reconciliation and Responsibility'. The intention was to consider the still–unpaid debt in the heart of America arising from the slave trade, the consequences of which had never been fully acknowledged, at least in the southern states.

I accepted an invitation from the Honorable Walter Kenny, the second African American holder of the office of Mayor of Richmond, to speak at the conference about Britain and Ireland. The organizers felt that there were some important and interesting parallels between the two situations. In particular, the issues of unacknowledged history and unhealed memories were felt to be powerful contributory factors in engendering present-day conflict, prejudice and bitterness.

While I was considering what I might say to such a gathering, an event occurred, very near Liverpool, which was to bring the horrors of Irish terrorism on to the television screens of every home in Britain.

3 *Enough is enough*

On 20 March 1993 the Provisional IRA planted two bombs in the centre of Warrington on a busy Saturday afternoon. Two boys were caught in the blast. Johnathan Ball, aged three and a half years, died instantly. Tim Parry, aged twelve, lived for five days. More than fifty other people were injured, some very seriously.

The indiscriminate nature of the attack, together with the ages of the two principal victims, provoked much outrage in the British media. It must be said, however, and this was generously acknowledged by Tim's father, Colin Parry, that many people in Ireland – the Republic and the North – had never received comparable coverage when their own loved-ones had been the victims of terrorist violence.

In the aftermath of Warrington, a group of women in Dublin, led by Susan McHugh, held peaceful demonstrations on the theme 'Enough is Enough'. The combination of an incident in Merseyside and a spontaneous movement for peace within Ireland seemed to provide the moment for which I had been waiting for some fourteen years, to express in a public way my own convictions. I wrote to the *Independent*, which published my letter on 29 March. I praised Susan McHugh's efforts, but urged people in Britain to recognise the background of the conflict, and our own historical responsibilities.

In my letter I pointed out some of the disasters of Irish history in which England had played a major part (see Appendix 1), and recalled Liverpool's close connection with them: in the Parochial Cemetery lie 100,000 victims of the famine in unmarked graves. The city's present population is fifty-one per cent Catholic, and well within living memory local elections were fought between Catholic and Protestant parties. This is the bitter context out of which has emerged the well-known ecumenism of our church leaders. I emphasized the need for us to look at causes, not merely at consequences. I suggested that it is never too late to say 'sorry', even at the risk of inviting accusations of handing victory to terrorists. Since forgiveness and reconciliation are at the heart of the gospel, the churches must have a part to play in this. The fears of both sides must be listened to carefully, since both Catholics and Protestants are victims. William Rathbone, a great Liverpool social reformer, once remarked, 'If a thing ought to be done, it can be done'. I asked whether, collectively or individually, we could find ways of making amends for the past, in order that a political solution for the North and South of Ireland might be achieved by consent.

Within a matter of days, the *Independent* received several letters, three of which were published. The most significant, and certainly the most unexpected, was from the former Chief of Staff, UK Land Forces, Major General Morgan Llewellyn, who had frequently served in Northern Ireland, and who was about to be ordained a deacon. In support of my position, he stated that the situation in Ulster is not essentially a military problem. Twenty years of service have come to nothing in the face of the intransigence of both sides. Only an act of sorrow and penitence by one side or the other can break the stalemate. 'It is not a weakness but a strength to admit to the errors of history and to exorcise the past so as to be able to work for reconciliation in partnership.' He called upon the British government to declare a carefully formulated policy for peace which would acknowledge the obligations that our history in Ireland, the Empire and NATO place upon us – a policy that should be properly resourced. And he called upon the churches to acknowledge the fact that they had been hijacked and exploited in the conflict. 'They should come together, without denying the richness of the variety of their religious expression, as members of the universal church of Christ to publicly proclaim the determination of all who call themselves Christians to join together in burying the past and building the future . . .'[1]

I imagined that that letter, and the other published ones, powerful as they were, would probably be the end of the matter. I was wrong. I began to receive letters myself, from all parts of Britain – more than two hundred in the following weeks. The *Irish Times* and a Belfast paper also carried my letter, and people wrote from both parts of Ireland. With very few exceptions – six, I think –

every letter was constructive. Of the six, one contained a razor-blade and offensive pastings of newsprint; another was a padded envelope. I thought it was a soft book, but it contained excrement.

I reached two conclusions. First, there is a substantial body of opinion in the United Kingdom which is, to say the least, uneasy about Britain's record in Ireland, and would like to see some form of apology and recompense. Second, within the island of Ireland, and from within both traditions, there is an amazing degree of gratitude extended towards anybody who tries to understand the difficulties faced by people there.

Many letters moved me profoundly, and were the principal reason for my deciding to go more deeply into these issues, and indeed to attempt to write this book. The abuse indicated what I already knew: that there are also people who are full of fear and insecurity, and who therefore feel themselves unable to engage in rational argument.

At the same time, the 'phone-in programmes on BBC Radio Merseyside were occupied for several days with 'the Irish question', and I was interviewed at length for RTE (the main Irish network), BBC Radio Ulster and Radio 4. It had become plain that, in giving expression to my personal convictions, I had unwittingly struck a chord with a great many people, and that, although there were those who asked God to forgive me for my uninformed and dangerous troublemaking, there was a consensus that historic wrongs needed to be put right. There was also an expressed desire to learn more about the history of our two islands.

Certain themes emerged. Members of the Church of Ireland, in the North and the Republic, expressed disquiet at what I had written. One, from County Antrim, expressed this movingly:

> I grew up taking privilege for granted. I have a great deal to learn about my own personal responsibility for bridging the chasms, both protestant and catholic and on a class basis, within our own protestant community. [This] has led to establishing friendships on a personal basis with people ranging from [a unionist politician] to Sinn Fein.

Many of my correspondents were very harsh in their judgements of Britain's conduct, particularly during the past twenty-five years. One, from south east London, put it starkly:

As a nation, we have yet to admit to our own policies of 'ethnic cleansing'. The British people will have to choose . . . . Either we continue to keep a stiff upper lip, as we are bled white by a civil war in our land, or we take the chance to heal the old wounds that fuel the bitterness. Compared to the present suffering, it will cost us nothing but our pride.

A common thread among English, Welsh and Scottish letters was a perceived need for England to shed the false ideals, values and national self-image which its imperial past had engendered. One, indeed, felt that the Irish question might become the catalyst for a redemptive process of national repentance.

A correspondent from Surrey expressed the thoughts of many when she pointed out that, although Northern Ireland seemed very remote from her tranquil village, she and many of her friends felt keenly the need to pray and search for a way to express penitence. Most of the letters agreed with the premise which I and Major-General Llewellyn had advanced, namely that no political solution was likely to succeed without the deep hurts of history being first acknowledged and then, if possible, healed.

A correspondent from West Yorkshire wrote:

My heart is filled with joy at your letter. The seventy year cloud over Ireland will lift, but before that, the British Government will have in penitence to ask the Irish Government for forgiveness for all the wrongs that have been done to the Irish over a long period of time. Then the Irish Government would ask forgiveness for all the things they have done wrong towards this country.

Among various suggestions of a practical nature, many were anxious to explore ways in which the North's endemic suspicion of the South might be addressed. This could involve the Republic dropping its territorial claims to Ulster, and explicit reassurance by the South that any future scheme of union (which most regarded as both logical and, in the fullness of time, inevitable) must make clear the separation between civil legislation and the teaching of the Roman Catholic Church. Certain civil liberties, which are enshrined in law in Britain, would also need to be safeguarded. Then, wrote a Lancashire correspondent, 'perhaps both states would be enabled to acknowledge that the past is the past, that truth, not myth and counter-myth, must prevail and that both sides genuinely seek mutual forgiveness and reconciliation.'

Several letters from Ireland, and a few from Britain, made reference to the Irish problem as essentially a British one. This was well expressed by a lady in Dublin:

> The English are not awfully good at drawing lines on maps. Every single time they have done it, there followed incredible civil strife . . . English people claim part of Ulster is as 'British' as Hampshire. I do not believe the decent people of Hampshire would allow discrimination on the basis of which way one worships. Yet successive British governments have upheld a corrupt 'statelet' since Lloyd-George told his famous lie to John Redmond.

There was a thread of personal guilt running through many of the letters. In some cases this had its roots in family history; in others, with no claims to Irish connections, in an inability to deal with feelings of vengeance and hatred. One lady (again from Surrey) wrote that she had prayed in anguish for feelings of revenge to be overcome in her life, especially after the bombing of the Household Cavalry in Hyde Park in 1981: 'The answer came: sort out the nail-bombs in your own life first . . .'

Some people who wrote, especially from Ireland, referred to particular instances of what they described as treachery by Britain in the very recent past. References were made to MI5, specific scandals and cover-ups; unwillingness to prosecute members of the security forces for inflicting harsh and unnecessary pain and sensory deprivation on unconvicted prisoners; interference in the due process of law; and much more. 'Bloody Sunday' in 1972, and the subsequent Widgery Report on the incident, were a recurring source of bitterness and resentment.

Members of Parliament also wrote to me. A Labour MP believed that the Christian solution — sadly overlooked by many politicians

– is sooner or later going to be the only way we can extricate ourselves from the mess. The basic feelings of a Conservative MP
were that 'the campaign of national apology is a good thing at the
right time' but that it would be seen in the context of terrorism,
so that politicians might find it difficult to support. It would be
vehemently opposed by the unionists and cause considerable
trouble within the Conservative Party.

Two letters, from the many I received, moved me very much.
It would be less than fair to the writers to attempt to summarize
them: they must be allowed to speak for themselves. The first
came from a resident of an old people's home in Bristol.

I am an 'O.A.P.', the descendant of the Scottish Protestant
colonists of the late 17th century whose family lived for 4
generations in Co. Antrim, on land taken by force from the
rightful Irish owners. In the middle of the last century, circumstances considered unfortunate by my Great-grandfather forced
the whole family to emigrate to Newfoundland. For myself, I
thank God that no relatives of mine now occupy land which
rightfully belongs to Eire.

Britain has gradually come to see that she can no longer hold
on to [territories taken from the indigenous peoples over 400
years] and after due shared-planning they have been handed
back, viz India, Rhodesia/Zimbabwe etc. etc. In 1997 Hong
Kong will be returned to China – and great is the problem of
achieving this. Yet it must be so.

Honourable consideration [must be given] to fixing a date
for returning Ulster to Ireland. Until this is done, and Britain
finally relinquishes all claim to Northern Ireland, the terrorists
of both sides will never stop their mutual hatred and murder,
aggravated as it is by religious uncontrollable hate. That bitterness is not felt by ordinary decent people in Northern Ireland,
who are in a majority, and who, of whatever race or denomination . . . openly declare 'Terrorists do not represent us.'

After all, English and Scottish people in Eire are living
unmolested lives precisely because Dublin governs, and her
honour is satisfied. I believe the same state of mutual and peaceful tolerance would pertain in the North too, provided that all

the people of the North were fairly represented in the Irish parliament in Dublin.

We have done enormous and shameful wrongs to the Irish. Now let us make amends, and do a great right.

The second letter was from Hampshire:

May I give you a story from my own family? An ancestor of mine was a landowner in Carlow, and a member of the protestant ascendancy, in about the year 1810. One night he was entertaining friends to dinner, when it came to his ears that his butler, a catholic as were all his servants, was in some way plotting against him. He looked round the table and realised that the magistrates of the town of Carlow were there in numbers enough to form a court. This they promptly did. They called the butler in, tried him, found him guilty, and hanged him forthwith at the rear of the mansion. There was no representation and no appeal, even to Dublin, let alone Westminster.

As a child of seven I was first introduced to that story as proof that catholics were never to be trusted. In four generations it had become a legend. Only later did it occur to me that the trial was by kangaroo court, and that the same story would lose nothing in the telling as it was passed on to the butler's descendants.

You are absolutely right. There seems to be in the English ruling mind an inability to acknowledge mistakes and injustice and to repent of them. To say sorry is not to condone the evil deeds of the I.R.A. or the U.F.F., but it might put us on the road to mutual forgiveness and understanding.

These, and many other letters, were sent to me as a result of just one letter which was printed in three newspapers. They reveal, I believe, a hitherto largely unexpressed awareness among ordinary people – in Ireland, as one might expect, but also in Britain – that the time has come for change. There has emerged, especially in England, a latent energy which, if it could be co-ordinated towards projects of reconciliation, would be formidable indeed. Many others have said that they would help if only they knew how, 'but what could we achieve on our own?'

A recurring theme is the widespread ignorance of Irish and British-Irish history: hence my attempt to produce an outline as an appendix to this book. Such an enterprise is open to criticism, not least on grounds of superficiality, but so much published history on this subject is daunting for non-specialist readers. These, however, are the very people who took the trouble to write to me after Warrington, and who feel in their hearts that there must be a better way.

4 *A still-unpaid debt*

The *Independent* letter and its aftermath led me to think more deeply about the bitter legacy which, I concluded, had been bequeathed by Britain to the Irish people. This became a more urgent preoccupation as I began to receive invitations to speak and write on the subject.

I had become accustomed to accusations of naiveté and political interference, and also to a deep sense of pessimism in the minds of many people – a belief that there could be no solution to 'the Irish question'. Others were more encouraging. A priest from Zimbabwe, the Revd Donald Bird, wrote how, after a vicious and bloody war, which might have soured relations between the races for years to come, the alternatives were spelled out on Independence Day 1980 by the Prime Minister, Robert Mugabe: hatred or reconciliation. He argued for the latter, and it worked. This experience showed that 'reconciliation is neither naive nor impossible. What has been done here can also be done in Ireland, given good will and a determination on all sides to make it work.'[1]

That very much accorded with my own views, but it became clearer to me that nothing could be gained by glossing over the 'difficult' parts of our shared story. Indeed, it was important for me to reflect on the grounds for my own feelings of disquiet and shame. These may be summarized thus:

1. We invaded Ireland, and fought our own battles there.
2. We robbed the Irish people of their language and their literature, and attempted to rob them of their church.
3. We colonized Ireland with foreigners, and persecuted the Irish people when they would not conform to our religion.
4. We drove the Roman Catholics into exile, and killed thousands of men, women and children; and we invoked God as our justification.

5. We failed to feed a starving people whose country was politic- ally part of our own, leaving millions to die or emigrate with- out hope. (There are perhaps one and a half million graves in Ireland to this day, unremembered, unprayed over, and unclaimed by anyone.)
6. We degraded the Irish people by caricaturing them in the British press and media.
7. When they protested, we met violence with violence.
8. These atrocities were not confined to the native Irish. When it suited our purpose, we 'planted' the land with Protestants, took advantage of their loyalty, and then told them we no longer needed them.

HISTORY NEED NOT BE LIVED AGAIN

In the middle of 1993, I received an invitation to speak to a pub- lic meeting in Dublin, sponsored by the Irish National Congress. This organization was described as 'a non-party political organiza- tion committed to work actively for the re-unification of Ireland through peaceful means'. It was explained that its members came from most political parties, the trade union movement, the pro- fessions and from all walks of life, including some members who were unemployed.

A friend in Dublin advised me to have nothing to do with them. My ordained colleagues at Liverpool Parish Church, with whom I discussed the invitation, felt rather differently. They made the very reasonable observation that I could hardly keep asking them to pray that God would use me, and then refuse at the first hurdle. Thus encouraged, I set off for Dublin.

The meeting was held in a packed trade union hall. It was clear that the sympathies of the INC would be nationalist, and I won- dered how a Church of England priest would be received. Although the large and enthusiastic audience was, indeed, parti- san, they were good listeners, and prepared to look at painful and difficult issues in an open and honest way.

The two other speakers with whom I shared the platform were Dr Brian Murphy, a Benedictine monk from Glenstal Abbey, and Father Joseph McVeigh, a parish priest from County Fermanagh.

Brother Brian traced the history of the Northern Ireland state from the Home Rule Act of 1912, through the Government of Ireland Act, 1921, to the present day. His conclusion, which was closely argued, with a wealth of quotation, was unequivocal. Justice, and the peace which might follow, could never be found in a partitioned Ireland. There had to be a better way of reconciling the unionist aspiration for Britishness with the nationalist aspiration for unity.

Fr McVeigh pulled no punches. He began with the Old Testament imperative to free the oppressed. He went on, sparing us few nasty details, to speak of the oppression of Catholic people in the north east, and the failure of the church to defend its own from 'British death squads'. He gave details of incidences of torture by the RUC; the mocking of Mass cards; derision of the Pope; and children threatened and abused by soldiers, who were then not punished. He described Catholics who prospered and flourished in the North, and turned their backs on their compatriots, as 'appeasers'. He continued: 'There will be no peace with partition. We must have freedom, unity and sovereignty.'

By this time, the audience was quite excited, and I felt very apprehensive. I need not have worried. I explained that I had come in response to their invitation, and that I was an Englishman, who had no intention of denigrating my country or apologizing for my nationality. In any case, my four grandparents had been English, Irish, Scottish and German!

Referring to the previous speaker's contribution, I said I could neither confirm nor condone what I had heard, but that it had shocked me deeply. In my prepared paper, I argued that it was too easy to throw bits and pieces of history at each other, in order to bolster up existing prejudice. History had to be studied, in all its complexity, before it could be set aside. Failure to do so had resulted in a vicious circle of bitterness, and political attempts, by Britain at least, to deal with consequences rather than with the root causes of conflict. I quoted some words of Maya Angelou, which I have found deeply inspiring:

> History, despite its wrenching pain,
> Cannot be unlived, but if faced
> With courage, need not be lived again.[2]

Facing the past in this way made it possible to acknowledge that terrible things have been done on all sides - violence, after all, begets violence, and blood will have blood. This assumption about fallen humanity is, indeed, the reason for my conviction that only the Christian gospel can provide the possibility of a way through, with Christ's teaching about forgiveness of enemies, and the importance of reconciliation, at its heart.

In Ireland, the consequences of British rule over the centuries are still apparent, both in the six counties which remain part of the United Kingdom, and the remaining twenty-six which do not. That is the context within which an agenda of sorrow and penitence, in hope of reconciliation, has to be worked out.

It was important for me to go to Dublin and to experience, for the first time at first hand, the depth of feeling among convinced nationalists about Britain's role in history, and (as it turned out) in the present, too. I was encouraged by the large number of young people, especially students, who, in discussion, said they were eager to hear all sides of the Northern Ireland question, and who told me that their historical studies had been as one-sided as I claimed mine were. They were willing to face with courage some of the pain, and to welcome into their midst a stranger from a very different tradition. It was a worthwhile expedition, and a very good omen.

AN UNUSUAL EXERCISE IN HONESTY

My next port of call was Richmond, Virginia, to take part in the conference 'Healing the Heart of America'. Six hundred delegates came together, from twenty countries and thirty cities in the United States.[3]

The premise was that racial distrust, resentment and fear are at the core of the crisis facing American cities. They permeated the national agenda: 'a continuing agony that stems from the fact that two peoples, Native and African Americans, were denied the freedom and dignity that the founders of the country claimed to cherish. White denial and guilt, and black anger, combine to produce name-calling, finger-pointing or silence. There is a massive failure to communicate.'

I had been asked to speak about Britain and Ireland – in particular, the benefits that might arise from addressing a bitter historical legacy with openness and honesty. There was a deep sense among many at Richmond, from their own American experience, that present-day politics were fuelled by wounds which were unacknowledged, and therefore unhealed.

The institution of slavery, and the racial pejudice which was its legacy, were founded on a blind and instinctive assumption that white was superior, and black to be feared. Such attitudes were bequeathed to subsequent generations, so that, today, many people in the United States have little capacity to feel the reality of what life was like for bonded Americans then, or for their descendants now. Richard Ruffin, who described himself as a direct descendant of the firebrand who fired the first shot in the Civil War, put it like this:

> Those who saw blacks as property did little to pass on to their children a positive idea of what blacks could contribute to American thought, politics, business and culture. An image was projected of black people as intellectually and morally inferior. People like myself need nothing less than a revolution of rising expectations for African Americans.

That speaker had begun a journey which was both painful and costly, but he concluded that real change was only possible after some such process of discovery. For me, the parallels with Britain and Ireland were striking. Unwillingness to face up to our shared history, in all its complexity, means that people and communities are locked into systems of prejudice, mistrust and low or non-existent expectation. It becomes impossible to think or speak well of the other.

In the predominantly Christian assembly at Richmond, I felt it right to draw upon the wisdom of the Bible, in particular the First Epistle of Saint John: 'In love there is no room for fear; indeed, perfect love banishes fear . . . But if someone says "I love God" while at the same time hating his fellow-Christian, he is a liar' (1 John 4.18-20). I tried to show how very difficult that text is for me, as an English Christian. I had been content to tolerate the hatred and the bloodshed, and the terrible complacency which has characterized Britain's relationship with Northern Ireland and its peoples in my own lifetime. At the same time, listening to many people speaking of the corrosive effect of racial prejudice on American society, I was forced to reflect, from the perspective of ministry in inner south London and in Liverpool, that racism is endemic in our land, too. Low expectations of those of other ethnic origins continue to permeate British society at every level.

As for Ireland, we have found it extraordinarily difficult to acknowledge the plank in our own eye, whilst being ready and eager to pronounce upon Bosnia, South Africa, Rwanda, and to demand an apology from Japan for its treatment of our people in the Second World War. My contribution at Richmond was to suggest that sorrow and penitence, in genuine hope of reconcili-ation, might provide a way forward: sorrow and penitence, appro-priately expressed, and backed up by real generosity in action.

In Richmond, there were many moments to treasure. One, in my own discussion-group, seemed to show just how much we have to undo, but how near at hand are the means towards under-standing. An African American doctor in his mid-seventies struck up a conversation with a white retired businessman of about the same age. The forebears of one had been slaves, and of the other, slave-owners. The doctor asked, 'How did you feel when you passed our homes on the way to school, when you saw us with-out shoes. You must have noticed how we lived?' He replied, 'Sir, I was not *allowed* to notice.'

The experience of Dublin and Richmond was both depressing and uplifting. In each case there was a willingness – eagerness, even – to seek new ways forward, and to be ruthlessly honest about the difficulties. At the same time, a sense of belief in the possibility of effecting change sent us away, as we say in Liverpool, with hope in our hearts. I was not even disconcerted when a very large lady from Alabama came up to me after my address, and said, 'Sir, with that accent, you could have read us the weather fore-cast, and we'd still have clapped.' As I left, I remembered some wise words of Bishop Hugh Montefiore: 'What may seem a shambles and a mess can become the springboard for wisdom and happiness, and the grace of God.'[4]

5 *Best purposes out of worst nightmares*

The consequences of the bomb in Warrington have been far-reaching. The Warrington Project has been established to promote reconciliation between the town and the people of Ireland, North and South. Its initial aim was to help people in the town, who had been deeply shocked by the tragic event, to understand something of the situation in Ireland, and to form a basis on which bridges of friendship and reconciliation might be built The conference which inaugurated the project, on 9 October 1993, was attended by the President of Ireland, Mary Robinson, the Prince of Wales, the Secretary of State for Northern Ireland and the Irish Ambassador. The President had also attended a memorial service for Johnathan and Tim in the local parish church.

The Warrington Project is an attempt to bring good out of evil, and to respond constructively to the deaths of two of the town's very young citizens. It is a long-term undertaking, and seeks to promote mutual understanding by establishing joint projects with Ireland and Northern Ireland, involving young people in schools, especially in the early years; training, especially in local government; and exchanges between religious, cultural and sporting groups. By these and other means, the project aims to break down traditional prejudice and unhelpful stereotypes.

President Robinson, in launching the Warrington Project, set the tone for its continuing work. She spoke of the true spirit of Ireland, and the revulsion felt by ordinary Irish people at the taking of lives for political ends. She told how 'the troubles' had claimed more than 3,000 lives in Northern Ireland since 1969, and how more than 30,000 people had been injured. A further 200 had lost their lives in related violence elsewhere. 'Warrington has been drawn into its own best purposes by our own worst nightmares.'[1]

The President gently pointed out that the massive media attention on Warrington was not matched by similar coverage of

Northern Ireland's own tragedies, and that this had led, in some quarters, to a kind of fatalism. For this reason, any moves towards reconciliation must take into account the pain of bereaved families and communities in Ireland as well. Through common pain might grow real understanding. In particular, she was anxious to stress the need for people in Britain to understand the extent of alienation between Catholic and Protestant communities in the North. A programme of 'Education for Mutual Understanding' which was in place in Northern Ireland might perhaps be copied in Britain, for 'our children are our future'.

It was necessary for all to understand that tolerance is the key to mutual respect and knowledge. Without it, people would remain trapped in historical antagonisms. For that reason, Warrington's aim – a seemingly modest but important one – must be to listen, and to seek real understanding through pain.

Colin Parry, Tim's father, who, with his wife Wendy, has worked tirelessly to build bridges of understanding, responded to the President's words by saying that he truly believed that good can come out of evil, and all must work to make it a reality. Politicians and church leaders must not be allowed to rest between atrocities, but must be urged to strive constantly to find new ways forward.

Warrington, and the conference which launched its project, prompted reflection on the bitter legacy of history, to which many of the contributors referred. It seems odd to the English mind that terrible events which occurred perhaps centuries ago should continue to be a factor in present-day conflict, but they are. It is primarily history, rather than present grievances, which has led young men to join what they perceive to be an armed struggle, and it is historical events which provide the focus for provocative celebrations, especially in the Protestant community.

That is why it is most important that we in Britain should learn much more about our common history, and why the emphasis which Warrington has placed upon education is so soundly based. But no less important are the simple human encounters which the project is facilitating. Much learning and mutual encouragement must grow from the simple human processes of meeting, friendship and discovery.

The Revd Stephen Kingsnorth, a Methodist minister in Warrington (and, incidentally, a former member of the Liverpool City Centre Ecumenical Team), has visited Ireland several times on behalf of the Warrington Project. He spoke at a large ecumenical service in Dun Laoghaire, and wrote about it subsequently to the *Irish Times*:

> We are not so foolish in Warrington as to believe that all atrocity and violence within the Anglo-Irish situation would cease at Bridge Street [where the bombs had been planted], but that does not nullify our belief that Warrington may yet be a watershed. Just as Enniskillen plumbed depths, because of remembrance, a nurse and a grieving father, so Warrington featured Mothers' Day, two innocents, and a dignified, visionary parental response. Many of us are only too well aware of the need for repentance by all. There have been atrocities committed in the past by all. Near Bridge Street is a statue of Oliver Cromwell, a man who, in a previous age, visited horrible massacre upon the people of Ireland. . . .
>
> When peace breaks out between Irish and British twinned towns, churches, communities, when reconciliation born of genuine penitence is forged, then perhaps present Northern communities will have a firmer rock on which to stand, and a friendlier community soup in which to share.
>
> For such relationships to bear fruit will take time. For those aspirations to find fulfilment in a way that starves violence of its motivating life force will take more time still. But that does not mean that Warrington and Peace 93 cannot be a watershed . . . We may be at the birth of a new process. The baby will have been growing secretly through gestation, and has many years to reach maturity. But it is born.[2]

GENUINE PENITENCE

Apart from the political moves towards what has come to be known as the peace process, and they are surely to be warmly welcomed, many people, both sides of the Irish Sea, have come to realize that there is indeed a better way. Stephen Kingsnorth used the significant phrase, 'reconciliation born of genuine penitence'. Penitence, or repentance, is a religious concept, a theological proposition. Both in theological and psychological terms, it is an essential prerequisite for reconciliation.

Repentance and reconciliation are part and parcel of the same process, and one is impossible without the other. If Saint John is right to say that perfect love casts out fear, then the removal of fear must be the aim of all parties to the Northern Ireland conflict. This can only happen, as Archbishop Robin Eames has written, by seeing reconciliation, not as a fact but as a process. He writes of the cumulative effect of changing attitudes by individuals and institutions – the removal of the more obvious causes of conflict and injustice in either community, and a willingness to see social wrongs in another locality as quickly as we can identify them in our own.[3]

A fruit of the dialogue which was begun at Warrington has been the discovery of just how infuriating to people in the Republic of Ireland is the (usually unconscious) sense of superiority which is displayed this side of the Irish Sea: 'If only they were more like us . . .' It is both insensitive and patronizing to suggest that 'we' know what is best for 'them'. Indeed, such thinking has soured Britain's relationship with Ireland, first as a colony and then as an independent state, over many centuries. That is why the utmost sensitivity is required, and why a genuine expression of sorrow and penitence may be the key to lasting progress.

It would mean acknowledging that we have had the major part in creating the mess in Ireland and that it involves us all. We do not know the answer, but we do have a sense that politics is not enough, because at the heart of the problem is fear and distrust and bitterness.

This is to suggest that a genuinely Christian insight might be brought into discussion of Britain's relationship with the island of Ireland. As Father Bird wrote, from Zimbabwe, this is more than a hopeless gesture. Penitence and reconciliation are neither unthinkable, nor naive. Who, after all, could have imagined that Sadat would sit down with Begin, De Klerk with Mandela, Rabin with Arafat? With God, all things are possible.

In Ireland, more than eighty per cent of the population claim allegiance to one or other Christian church. It may not be fanciful to suggest, therefore, that an approach in Christian terms might receive a ready welcome. Indeed, conversations which I have had with people from both the main religious and political traditions, and in both parts of Ireland, suggest that an expression of sincere penitence for the past would be very welcome indeed, and could make possible an entirely different atmosphere for future discussion. Indeed, just such an expression by the Archbishop of Canterbury in Dublin in November 1994 received massive coverage in the media in the Irish Republic, though it was scarcely mentioned in Britain.[4]

Such an approach would require, this side of the Irish Sea, the greatest humility, and the kind of honesty which was displayed in a previous age by people such as Wilberforce and Shaftesbury. They, and other Christian reformers like them, were prepared to spell out the implications of a truly Christian faith, and to accept ridicule for so doing. That is often the lot of prophets.

Genuine penitence would involve taking seriously the implications of our common Christian heritage, and Christ's challenge to all people of good will, to accept responsibility for what has been done, and thereby to make, and to urge upon our leaders, a new beginning. This would have implications for the way we act towards those we believe have been wronged, for penitence and reparation are interwoven. The tremendous service which the Warrington Project has done has been to show that, in Mary Robinson's words, the best purposes *can* come out of the worst nightmares. Not for nothing did Jesus say that it is the peacemakers who are blessed (Matt. 5.9).

6 *Swords into ploughshares*

In May 1994 I began four months of study leave, which I was able to spend largely in Ireland, listening, reading and writing – a rare luxury. Before setting down some of the events and conversations I had during that period, it seems right to stand back from this personal record, and take stock.

My initial convictions about the need for sorrow and penitence remained undiminished – indeed, they had been enhanced by all that had happened and all that I had seen and heard. I have already indicated that the concept of penitence is a spiritual one, but it may also bear upon what an Irish church leader called 'the real world we have to inhabit over here'.

These verses from chapter four of the Book of Micah will be familiar to many, with their idealistic vision of peace and justice:

> For out of Zion shall go forth the law, and the Word of the Lord from Jerusalem.
>
> He shall judge between many peoples, and shall decide for strong nations afar off;
>
> and they shall beat their swords into ploughshares, and their spears into pruning hooks;
>
> nation shall not lift up sword against nation, neither shall they learn war any more;
>
> for they shall sit every man under his vine and under his fig tree, and none shall make them afraid;
>
> for the mouth of the Lord of Hosts has spoken.
>
> For all the peoples walk each in the name of its god, but we will walk in the name of the Lord our God for ever and ever. (Mic. 4.1–5)

The prophet speaks of peace and justice. His is a vision of nations which no longer settle disputes by means of violence, and of peoples who live without fear and who walk in God's ways. It is not a prophecy with an immediate reference, but looks forward to the days to come. In the meantime, God's people are to pray, to struggle and to long for peace and justice. For Christians, the imperative has an added urgency, for the Lord tells us that the peacemakers are especially blessed.

In arguing for sorrow and penitence as the only way to lasting peace in Ireland, I do not advocate a United Ireland, or a strengthened union or any other political consequence – that is not my concern. The process of repentance is crucial *for its own sake,* without prejudice to present or future political initiatives. We as English people can claim no interest in Irish affairs unless by penitence, humility and love we begin to heal the wounds of history, and become better friends with our Irish neighbours. That is the beginning.

Of all the people who have written or spoken about Ireland, none has done so with greater passion than Cardinal Henry Manning. To read his words, more than a century later, is to be reminded that Manning was a true visionary. It is sad that history has regarded him less than kindly, perhaps because of his controversial utterances, and his uncompromising views on such matters as papal infallibility. He was ordained an Anglican priest and became Archdeacon of Chichester in 1840. From that conservative, impeccably English beginning, he converted to Roman Catholicism in 1851, and later, as Archbishop of Westminster, became a fearless champion of the rights of the Irish people, and a sharp thorn in the side of the British Establishment. He wrote these words, of Ireland: 'To our own hurt, we have made the English name hateful in the past, and we must bear the penalty until we have repaid the wrong . . . We English can be cool and calm about the matter, but we must not forget that the accumulated animosity of the past is born in the blood of Irishmen.'[1]

Don Simpson, who has done much to 'rehabilitate' Manning, has written:

> Of all Englishmen of his time, and even since, Manning came nearest to understanding and healing the situation. Politicians and military men have tried their best, but they have not gone to the deeper roots of the conflict, the unhealed wounds of

centuries, nor to the deeper cure, in mutual repentance, forgiveness and renewal under God.[2]

Difficult as it is, we have to be prepared to face our history,
however strong may be our personal inclination to disown it. We
in this country are woefully ignorant of the history of Ireland,
even basic historical events, let alone their context, and that makes
intelligent analysis of the present situation very difficult. It is not
easy to find comprehensive courses in Irish history in British uni-
versities, which makes the Institute of Irish Studies in the
University of Liverpool particularly important. The situation in
our schools is little better. The Roman Empire, the French
Revolution and the American Civil War claim higher priority
in the curriculum than the island and peoples to which we are
closest, in geography, faith and language.

I realize that many people, including those who care most
deeply about Ireland, believe that history should be set aside –
'there's too much of it'; I realize, too, that in a sense there is no
such thing as history – there are events, which in the fullness of
time become overlaid with myth and culturally-determined inter-
pretation.

But if we are, in Mannings words, to repay the wrong, or to
heal the wounds, then it is absolutely essential that we revisit past
events, and, with as much objectivity as we can muster, interrogate
the historical records. Only thus can we begin to understand, and
to pray and work with intelligence rather than mere emotion. It
is plain that terrible things have happened in Ireland from the end
of the twelfth century to our own. I believe it is fair to say that
Britain has consistently been prepared to use Ireland and its
people, in what we now know as the North and the Republic, for
its own advantage; and because of the terrible suffering which has
ensued down the centuries, must be seen as the principal architect
of Northern Ireland's present trauma. Sir Patrick Mayhew's
measured words come nearer to acknowledging that reality than
those of any other recent British politician: 'There is much in the
long and often tragic history of Ireland for deep regret.'[3]

To say this is not to suggest that all the horrors were one-sided:
violence and bitterness always breed the same; nor that there were

not cogent political reasons for decisions which were taken. The point is that history has to be revisited and interpreted if we are to understand that present dilemmas have their roots in past events and decisions. To those who say 'It's all in the past, why rake over past embers,' I would quote from a private letter from a former republican terrorist, who is now just as vehemently opposed to a United Ireland. He wrote: 'It is not present-day injustice which fuels the conflict in this land. Enormous progress has been made in the last twenty years in redressing the balance between our two communities. The real trouble is Cromwell and King Billy, and nobody knows how to bury them.'

But, some may feel, terrible as the story has been, it is not our fault. We had no part in Ireland's tormented past. Maybe not, but we cannot escape the results, nor a measure of moral responsibility. The curse of the troubles hangs over all of us, as do the consequences of British rule over the centuries. We cannot live in the past, but unless we find a way of owning past deeds, unless we can discover some corporate sense of responsibility based on our common humanity, as well as nationality, then we shall be led – as I believe successive British Governments have been – to tinker with consequences instead of addressing causes.

The film *Schindler's List* has led to some anguished heart searching in Germany about the Nazi era. Present day Germans were not responsible, yet a man of mixed German and Jewish ancestry can write:

> If the entire German people, past and present, is not collectively guilty of what happened at Auschwitz and elsewhere – and that is an absurd charge to make – it is certainly true that German History, particularly, and European civilization generally, must bear this awful stain until the end of time.[4]

But when we have revisited past events, sifted and considered them as best we can, what then? If we are Christians, of whatever tradition, whether by accident of birth, conviction or conversion, then we ought to be led to examine our need of personal and corporate repentance.

Alec Porter, who is descended from what he calls the old Church of Ireland ascendancy, which (he says) had introduced the

Penal Laws and deprived the native Irish of their land, their culture and their religion and had oppressed the Presbyterians in the North, goes on to say:

> I blamed the IRA and the Orangemen for their inherited attitudes, but it began to dawn on me that an unfaced and unexpressed sense of guilt, passed down over generations on one side, could be more responsible for sowing the seeds of violence than even an expressed sense of injustice passed down the generations on the other. An honest look at these things, and apology for them to God and to others – repentance if you like – brought me to a liberation from falsehood, and also a sense of forgiveness, a new comprehension that 'the truth shall set you free'. We need no longer be prisoners of history.[5]

THE HEART OF THE GOSPEL

It is a fact of Christian experience, but also true to human psychology, that there can be no reconciliation without sorrow and penitence. Christians therefore have to understand that repentance and reconciliation are the very heart of the gospel, and you cannot achieve one without the other. But if repentance is the only way to reconciliation, then we have to ask, repentance for what? As an Englishman and a priest in the Church of England, I should have to say that repentance is due for the English part in producing the present situation in Ireland – especially in the North – and for my personal complacency in the face of murder and mayhem. In repenting of all that, I am inescapably faced with the issue of forgiveness – my need to forgive others for words and evil deeds, but also, and more importantly, to ask forgiveness for myself and for my country. The plain though difficult truth is: repentance which wants to disclaim responsibility, repentance which still leaves room for self-justification is not Christian repentance at all.

There is an urgent need for British Christians to deepen their understanding of the conflicts in Ireland – the hatred, anger, insecurity and fear – and at the same time be ready to give thanks to God for all that is good and lovely in that land – its peoples, its cultures, and the richness of its contribution to Western civilization, out of all proportion to its size or population. And because politics is the way in which human affairs are shaped, we are to pray for politicians, British, Irish and Northern Irish, of whatever persuasion, because their limitations of vision, their human frailties, are the same as our own.

The first leader in the *Daily Mail* on 11 March 1994 referred to IRA mortar bombs which had been discovered at Heathrow Airport. The writer said that, if they had exploded, the victims would have had nothing to do with the miseries of Ireland. That is at one and the same time both true and untrue. We have to understand that ambiguity, to work with it, and to help others to do the same. Only by so doing can we bring closer that Day of the Lord for which Micah longed and Henry Manning worked, and which is God's promise for his people.

An ardent republican in Northern Ireland has written:

> We [the nationalist community] and they [our Protestant neighbours] must be ready to talk and apologise and unite, and the only way that can be achieved is through understanding. Are we ready for that painful experience? If we are not then we consign the people of this island to endless war.[6]

I believe repentance by the British nation and people is the one key which can unlock that process. It is for the churches to show the way.

7 *A bundle of prejudices*[1]

The conviction that Britain owes a debt of sorrow and penitence to the peoples of Ireland is the central preoccupation of this book. I have tried to set out some of the reasons for that conviction. However, the reaction of many people in Britain to such a notion is incredulity. I have already mentioned the razor-blades and the excrement from the lunatic fringe, but similar sentiments, even if they are expressed a little more decorously, are to be found in surprising quarters. A respected senior clergyman said to me, 'You're a bloody fool, Nicholas. You should learn to keep your mouth shut.'

I decided to send him the first draft of this chapter, in the hope that he might come to see that there may be more to what I am saying than mere eccentricity, and that it has an all-too-solid basis in reality. To date, the package has not been acknowledged, and my letter has gone unanswered, but such is the strength of feeling which this issue engenders, and the apprehension which so often seems to accompany serious thought.

In August 1993 I spent a couple of hours in Belfast with a television producer who was undertaking serious research into the great famine of the 1840s. He was interested in my ideas about the need for sorrow and penitence, and suggested that readiness to forgive is not uppermost in the British character. He cited, by contrast, the reconciliation that has occurred in Nigeria between the Ibo and Yoruba tribes, the extraordinary response to an appeal for reconciliation between black and white by the Prime Minister of Zimbabwe (to which I have already referred) and the unfolding of events in South Africa. On the basis of personal experience of working in Africa, he also dared to predict early reconciliation between Hutu and Tutsi in Rwanda.

There is something in the African psyche – I can't explain it, but we seem to have lost it. It is a capacity for charity and

generosity of spirit which is unforgettable when one has experienced it. You will find it very difficult to convince people
in England that you are engaged in anything more significant
than a middle class guilt-trip, but you are, and you must
prove it.

We talked about the famine, his particular line of interest. He
spoke sympathetically of the problems faced by the British government of the day – poor communications, the need to export
grain and livestock to maintain capital reserves, and he praised the
unprecedented nature of relief when it was given. He also referred
to the problems faced by some landlords, who had received no
rent for up to thirteen years. In short, he was prepared to make
every allowance for the actions of the government at the time of
the famine, with the benefit of hindsight and specialist knowledge.
But he went on:

> For all that, nothing can alter or excuse the brutal truth, that
> anti-Irish prejudice, and parsimony in high places, cost thou-
> sands and thousands of human lives. That is unforgivable,
> because it was deliberate. People lie buried all over Ireland, and
> some in Britain, without having received the dignity of
> Christian burial and without proper graves. That is so great an
> evil that anything which could be done to atone for such
> wickedness would be justified. You must go on urging an
> apology, at least.

Later he wrote to me, having discussed our conversation with
senior colleagues in London. 'The sad thing is that their reaction
to the idea of an apology being offered to the Irish people is one
of mild incredulity, even scorn. I try to explain that it all makes
more sense over here.'

We had concentrated in our conversation on the famine, but
that is just one event, albeit a defining one, in more than eight
centuries of conflict between our two islands. The 'incredulity
and scorn' which may be felt at the suggestion that Britain owes
an expression of penitence to the people of Ireland demands some
further evidence. The fact that the roots of this conflict lie deep
in history in no way diminishes the unease which we in Britain

ought to feel. It is the wrenching pain of history which continues to fuel the conflict in Northern Ireland and may yet undo the peace process. That history cannot be unlived, but unless it is faced with courage, we and the people of Ireland are doomed to endless repetition.

HUMOUR AND HATRED

Colin O'Brien Winter was consecrated Anglican Bishop of Damaraland (Namibia) in 1968. He was deported by the South African Government in 1972 for his outspoken and active opposition to apartheid. He spent the years of his exile touring the world, speaking and preaching against the iniquities of the system in South Africa. He pleaded for Christians in Europe and the United States to understand and identify with their oppressed sisters and brothers. He never spared himself, and died of heart failure – some said of a broken heart – at the age of fifty-three in 1981.

Colin was of English-Irish parentage and he never forgot what he called the crushing weight of history which bore down upon his Irish ancestors. He felt particularly keenly about the dispossession of the native Irish people, and the present-day indignity of what passes in England for humour about the Irish, but which is in reality a demeaning caricature. I remember a sermon which Colin preached in the parish in Peckham where I was a curate. He spoke about humour which is at the expense of other people or races, especially that which is directed against the Jewish people. Of such jokes, he said: 'They began in the Music Hall, but they ended in Belsen.'

He then made comparisons with Britain's treatment of Irish people.

> We have vilified and demeaned them, and we have made them the butt of jokes which, under the guise of 'taking the Mickey out of Paddy', are designed with one end in view. This is to portray all Irish people as feckless, stupid, and above all, socially and educationally inferior.[2]

The roots of this contempt go back a long way. From the twelfth century, English perceptions of the native Irish have been less than complimentary. One of the earliest and most influential visitors was the historian Giraldus Cambrensis, who travelled to Ireland in 1183, a period when Ireland was regarded throughout Europe as an influential centre of Christian civilization and learning. Doubtless King Henry II, to whom the writer's *History and Topography of Ireland* was dedicated, approved of the analysis:

> This is a filthy people wallowing in vice. They live on beasts only, and they live like beasts . . . They are treacherous and deceitful . . . They have not progressed at all from the primitive habits of pastoral living . . . Of all peoples it is the least instructed in the rudiments of the faith.[3]

Giraldus' history was quoted for centuries as fact by historians; it was published as late as Elizabeth I's reign. Much writing in the Elizabethan age sought to justify conquest and colonization, and portrayed the Irish as backward and barbarous – above all, in need of civilizing by the English. The Irish were not even good Catholics! Edmund Spenser described them as 'blindly and brutishly uninformed' in the faith. Furthermore, they were 'licentious, swearers and blasphemers, common ravishers of women, and murderers of children.'[4]

The only solution was to occupy the whole of the island by force, and educate and protect the people. Nathaniel Crouch wrote in 1693:

> The English endeavoured to civilise the people, and to introduce the English laws, language, habit and customs among them, thereby to reduce them to civility, yet such was their . . . implacable malice to the English . . . [that] they took all advantages, most perfidiously to rise up and imbrue their hands in the blood of their English neighbours, and Ireland hath long continued a true Aceldama, or field of blood, and a dismal sepulchre for the English nation.[5]

Faced with this kind of material, it is scarcely surprising that the Irish became the butt of humour. A collection of *Teagueland Jests and Bog Witticisms* in 1749 stated in its preface that 'Nothing more recommends Teague and his countrymen than their natural stupidity.'

The historian David Hume attributed the 'profound barbarism and ignorance' of the Irish to the fact that 'They were never conquered or even invaded by the Romans, from whom all the western world derived its civility.'[6] They had remained Catholic after, and in spite of, the Reformation, on account of their extreme rudeness and ignorance.

The notion that English rule was beneficial to the Irish was exploded by Jonathan Swift, who pointed out that it was, in reality, of immense benefit to England, and an unmitigated disaster for Ireland. In his famous satire, *Gulliver's Travels*, Swift wrote:

> Ships are sent with the first opportunity, the natives driven out or destroyed, their princes tortured to discover their gold; a free licence given to all acts of inhumanity and lust, the earth reeking with the blood of its inhabitants; and this execrable crew of butchers employed in so pious an expedition, is a modern colony sent to convert and civilise an idolatrous and barbarous people.[7]

Others took up similar themes. John Curry, in 1775, criticized British writers for presenting Irish history in terms of the crimes of the Irish people: 'Hence a system of plunder and persecution, organised into a code of laws, was excused, for defended it could not be . . . Insult was added to outrage. The Irish were considered scarcely human, and inhuman indeed was the system by which they were oppressed.'[8] In the same decade, Arthur Young wrote, prophetically:

> A better treatment of the poor in Ireland is a very material point to the welfare of the whole British Empire. Events may happen which may convince us fatally of this truth – if not, oppression must have broken all the spirit and resentment of men. By what policy the government of England can for so many years have permitted such an absurd system to be matured in Ireland, is beyond the power of plain sense to discover.[9]

With the arrival of Irish emigrants in Liverpool from the mid-nineteenth century, the local press fanned the flames of an already real prejudice in the Protestant citizens. The *Liverpool Mail* wrote in 1841: 'One of the most obnoxious vices of popery is that where it prevails, it generates hosts of filthy and importunate mendicants – the vermin of the human race.' And in 1847, during the great famine: 'The scum of Ireland come to Liverpool. Begging is their profession, the workhouse their retreat.'

The *Liverpool Mercury* in 1848 went further: 'There is a taint of inferiority in the character of the pure Celt which has more to do with his present degradation than Saxon domination.'

Stereotypes such as these were used as an excuse for England to involve itself in the affairs of the 'inferior' Irish. Otherwise discerning people were encouraged to believe that the poverty and appalling conditions of life in Ireland were the fault of the Irish themselves, and not caused, or at best exacerbated, by English policy and self-interest.

There were exceptions to this trend. Arthur Young, again, had struck a more perceptive note in 1780: 'It is an illiberal business for a traveller to sit down coolly in his closet and write a satire on the inhabitants of a country. Many strokes in [the Irish] character can be ascribed to the extreme oppression under which they live.'[10] Their virtues, he added, 'deserve attention at least as much as their failings.'

At the height of the Atlantic slave trade, however, *Punch* could still print lines like these, in 1818:

> Six foot Paddy, are you no bigger –
> You whom cozening friars dish –
> Mentally, than the poorest nigger
> Grovelling before fetish?
> You to Sambo I compare
> Under superstition's rule
> Prostrate like an abject fool.[11]

SECTARIAN STRIFE

It is hardly surprising that prejudice of this kind acquired a religious dimension. In Britain, it was the Irish who were abused and ridiculed. In Northern Ireland it was (and is) 'the Catholics', in spite of the fact that Protestants and Catholics alike had both suffered penalties, and jointly struggled for Irish independence in the late eighteenth century.

The ruling Protestant ascendancy was content to link religious prejudice with its own political objectives: hence 'Home Rule – Rome Rule', and legislation which denied Catholics equality of opportunity in jobs, housing and suffrage.

In 1933 Sir Basil Brooke, Prime Minister of Northern Ireland, said: 'There are a great number of Protestants and Orangemen who employ Roman Catholics. I feel I can speak freely on this subject as I have not a Roman Catholic about my own place. I would appeal to loyalists therefore to employ good Protestant lads and lasses.'[12]

Brian Faulkner, Northern Ireland's last Prime Minister, appealed to his fellow Protestants: 'Orangemen should be anxious to find employment for our brethren.'[13]

More recently, the Revd Ian Paisley has played upon the glories of the Protestant heritage. He declares himself 'For God and for Ulster'. At the same time, he states that the way to the land of gospel liberty has been blocked by 'Priestcraft, superstition and papalism, with all their attendant vices of murder, theft, immorality, lust and incest.'[14]

The logical outcome of this kind of rhetoric, and the cumulative effect of centuries of invective and propaganda, is that they fuel 'the armed struggle' on both sides, and lead to the battles of history being endlessly refought. In the case of the most extreme loyalist Protestants, a vicious diet of anti-Catholic propaganda which presents them as inferior, contemptible and untrustworthy, leads many to believe that it is almost a Christian duty to murder them. This is not because of their political aspirations, but simply because they are Catholics.

> If Taigs are made for killing,
> then blood is made to flow.[15]

'It began in the Music Hall, it ended in Belsen', said Bishop Colin Winter. In Ireland one might say that it began with England's need to present its Irish neighbours as irrational and innately prone to violence; it has continued until late 1994 on the streets of Belfast.

It is important that we should read material such as this, because it is all too easy to disregard the deep sense of hurt and insult which many Irish people feel. The fact that so many have settled happily in Britain, and contribute so much to our national life, does not make the often-quoted words of the Revd Sydney Smith any less true today than when he wrote them early in the nineteenth century: 'The moment the mere name of Ireland is mentioned, the English seem to bid adieu to common feeling, common prudence and common sense, and act with the barbarity of tyrants and the fatuity of idiots.'[16]

8 *A terrible betrayal*

During 1993–94 I have made four visits to Northern Ireland in order to meet, and most importantly listen to, as many people as possible. I have been particularly anxious to meet members of the unionist community, since they often feel unheard, or at best misunderstood, in England, and because they claim a special identity of relationship with Britain. Nearly everybody I approached was willing, and often anxious, to talk, and in some cases arranged gatherings of people to meet me.

The reporting of these conversations places me in a somewhat difficult position. People said what they felt because they trusted me. I should betray that trust if I revealed their identity, or even, in many cases, the location of their homes. What follows is as accurate a record of real conversations as my memory allows. I have not, except where it is necessary to record a piece of continuous dialogue, included my own questions or comments, and where I have, I have placed them in italics. I have also avoided the customary use of quotation marks.

A VERY MORAL SOCIETY

I spent an evening with a group of professional men and their wives in a town in the north east. They included business men, a Presbyterian minister, a senior police officer, a teacher, and others whose occupations I cannot remember. All were convinced unionists, and some of them active in the Unionist Party. My host had explained that I wanted to listen and learn. At first, conversation was difficult and stilted, but having wined and dined very well, they opened up.

What must we do to be understood? We have put up with so much. We've made mistakes – of course we have; who doesn't? We shouldn't have thrown out Sunningdale,[1] for example, in Heath's time. If we hadn't, we might have avoided twenty years of chaos. Now we're going to have to settle for much less. It's a damned shame.

We seem to get the blame for all Britain's faults, but I think it's because we're misunderstood. Perhaps we don't understand ourselves! For fifty years we had things very good here, I can't deny that. We were blind to the troubles of the Catholics because they didn't touch us personally, and in any case we believed Britain would always pick up the tab and look after us. What we're most afraid of now is losing our identity.

What do you mean by that?

Well, our Britishness. That's very important to us, the fact we're British.

I wonder exactly what you mean by that? Three of my grandparents, you see, were English, Scottish and Irish. That is how they would have described themselves. Those were their national identities.

Yes, Yes. But we are British. We owe allegiance to our Queen, and we gave our lives – thousands of them – in both wars. Who did we do that for?

That's a fair point, Tom, but actually, I wouldn't really object to being Irish, just so long as I could be British as well. I don't know the mainland, anyway. This is my home.

Ireland, you mean? Do you visit the Republic?

I do not, unless I have to. It's a foreign land.

Just suppose, for the sake of this discussion – hypothetically, if you like – that there was, in your lifetimes, a united Ireland, however arrived at. What do you think you would do?

Get out.

Stay and fight.

Reluctantly live with it.

Where would you go?

Britain, of course.

Who would you fight?

The Catholics. They're the cause of all this trouble, always were. Don't you know your history? And now Adams is getting the red carpet and cups of tea as if he was a hero! Of course I'd fight; so would you if you really understood, believe me.

Can you help me to understand what you think the unionist community really stands for? I mean, you're so often painted in negative colours.

You'll laugh at this . . .

I'm not hear to laugh, I'm here to learn.

Fair enough, then. But I'd have to say 'No Surrender' and curb the power of the Roman church. I know Paisley's made those into slogans about Rome Rule and all the rest, but that is our identity, our past, our Protestant heritage. We're proud of it. To you, 'No Surrender' probably sounds silly, but to us it's the one thing that really matters.

Well, I'd have to agree, but I don't think you've answered Nicholas's question, George, not really. I think he's looking for our good points, aren't you?

Well, I want to know what you think the unionist community really stands for, for better or worse.

I'll start: Pride.

Enterprise.

Hard work.

The Bible . . . Christian values.

Friendliness. We're a very friendly community.

Generosity.

Law and order.

Community, a sense of community, shared interests.

We've a right to be proud, so we have. You know, I think they envy us a bit, not for our past privileges, but because of who and what we are. I think we're being very honest with each other tonight, much more than usual. When did we last have a conversation like this? We avoid politics and religion like the plague, let's face it. Maybe we've been too afraid to talk about the good things, as if we hardly believed them.

I think there's something in that. There's so much that's good here, but Britain has never seen it – OK that may be down to us, but it's true – and I think we've been used. Used when it suits them, and now it doesn't, so they can leave us to sink or swim.

I don't think it'll come to that, myself. After all, we were here first.

I used to think that, but it's bunkum, you know. We drove the Irish out by force, on to land that wouldn't support animals. It's not surprising they're afraid of us.

Yes, but we had to get rid of them. They were violent and disloyal. Force was the only language they understood.

Do you think that justified Cromwell, the Penal Laws?

They applied to our people as well.

Anyway, that's all in the past. Now it's our turn to feel hard done-by.

What you've got to understand is this. I'm sorry to say it, but it's the truth. Catholics always have been, and always will be, disloyal.

Disloyal to what or to whom?

The Crown, of course.

All right. If (and we're speaking hypothetically), but if it's true that a majority of Roman Catholics in Northern Ireland feel no allegiance to the British Crown, have you ever stopped to consider why that might be?

It must be difficult for you as an outsider to understand.

I'm trying very hard to understand. Can't you help me? You've said some highly damaging things about the Roman Catholic community. I'm trying to tease out why you feel that way, or perhaps why they do.

I'm sorry. You've got a point, especially with the Penal Laws. I'm not surprised they hate the British. You wouldn't forget an experience like that, not in a small country like this; but the funny thing is, I don't believe they *do* hate us, not most of them. The government, yes; Stormont when we had it; but I don't think they hate us as people. Fact is, Britain has got an awful lot to answer for. I do know a bit of history. They've generally left Ireland to it's own devices. You've only got to remember the famine.

I wondered when that would come up.

It's the anniversary soon, isn't it? A hundred years.

Hundred and fifty, actually, Tom! 1845, 1995.

Oh well . . . In any case, it was an act of God and nobody's fault.

How very unfair to God! I don't mean the failure of the crop itself, that's not the point. It's what we were saying earlier: people had been forced on to such poor land that they could only grow spuds. Britain didn't *cause* it, of course, but I don't think they cared much when it happened. And now there are people, millions of them for all I know, stirring up trouble all over the world, especially America. They were forced to emigrate, Protestants as well. Now they're more Irish than the Irish.

I can't resist saying you're more British than the British!

Fair comment! I'm only saying the famine had terrible consequences.

Yes, it did. Time's getting on. Is there anyone who has not spoken yet who'd like to say something?

Thank you, Canon. I have not said anything so far, but I have listened with great care. I have found this whole evening very uncomfortable, because it has confirmed things I have been thinking for a long time. In my conscience I feel very unhappy about the legacy of Stormont, very unhappy about the way our Catholic neighbours have been treated here, unhappy as a Presbyterian at the way we have rejected dialogue, and very apprehensive about the future. The truth is that our government practised discrimination against its Catholic citizens: housing, jobs, even who they could vote for.

That didn't justify the violence, though, did it?

Well, violence is never right, but it's sometimes a last resort for desperate people.

Rubbish! All they wanted was a united Ireland, by force, and they'll get it, that's what makes me sick. The IRA have won, that's the plain truth. Violence does pay.

I should like to finish, if I may. I said I am uneasy in my conscience, and so I am. As a [Presbyterian] minister, I try to read the Scriptures each morning. The other day I read the story of the conversion of Cornelius and his household in Acts, chapter 10; at least, that's what I've always thought it was about. But it's not. It's about how *Peter* was converted to an understanding that the Good News is for *all* people, Gentiles as well as Jews. It could only happen when he was open to what God was saying to him. Can you see the connections? It's disturbed me very much. In a long ministry, I've scarcely had anything to do with Catholics. We felt we were the chosen ones. Now I feel very uneasy in my mind.

Oh, but you've had a wonderful ministry, Albert . . . That's a very moving story, but the point of this discussion is that we face a really desperate situation here. It's our whole way of life that we're talking about, not a party game.

Perhaps we ought to leave it there. It's nearly midnight. You've been very patient and courteous with me. Thank you very much.

Before we finish, Nicholas, I'd like to thank you for coming to listen to us. We live in very grave times. I heard this morning that recruitment of Protestant paramilitaries is at an all-time high since this Downing Street business. If you can help people to understand that, you will have done us all a favour. They're playing with fire. We're heading for civil war. Perhaps you'll remember to pray for us?

This conversation took place between highly articulate people. Many of the opinions expressed go to the heart of unionist concerns. Throughout the long evening there was a constant undercurrent of depression, and a sense of betrayal. There was also a curious inability, or unwillingness, to work out the implications of 'Britishness'; but it was a useful and revealing occasion, and, in the honesty and openness of that Presbyterian minister, a very moving experience.

I was struck by the man who said that they do not normally discuss such matters. As so often it needed the catalyst of an interested visitor to draw them out, and a degree of trust, which in this case was ensured by our host, who realized the importance of presenting the unionist case in a sensible way.

SCRIPTURAL VALUES

In another home I was invited to share a Bible study with a group of church-goers, most of them members of the (Anglican) Church of Ireland, but with a couple of Presbyterians present. After a period of general discussion about church life, and comparisons between our respective churches, I was invited to choose a text for discussion. I selected the passage from the First Epistle of St John, which I had used in Richmond, Virginia: 'In love there is no room for fear; indeed, perfect love banishes fear . . . If someone says "I love God" while at the same time hating his fellow-Christian, he is a liar' (1 John 4.18–20).

Do you think that verse is compatible with some of the attitudes towards Christians of other denominations which I have come across during my visit?

I think that's a very provocative introduction, if I may say so. You have to see these things in the right context.

I'm sorry; I didn't intend to be provocative. It struck me that this passage is very relevant to the situation here. It was addressed to people who were facing real difficulties, and were tempted to meet violence with violence. Surely that's relevant?

Well, I don't know how you can know that. The Bible witnesses against sin: sins like dishonesty, drink, gambling, sexual immorality, dishonouring the Sabbath, breaking God's Law. It shows us the better way, God's way. We are by and large a very moral society here, and scriptural values still matter to us.

Yes, we regard those things as very important, Protestants I mean.

Do you think Roman Catholics share those concerns?

Well, some would, I suppose.

That's not fair, you know. The Pope is very concerned about morality. Besides, my niece married a Catholic boy.

I'd no idea!

Yes, and he's a very nice lad. No problems at all.

What about the children?

They haven't got any yet, but they will work that out when it happens.

Perhaps . . . I'll tell you what I can't take: transubstantiation. It's blasphemous. Who could believe all that about the bread and wine changing? It's not natural.

Assuming, and it's a big assumption, that most modern Catholics hold that particular doctrine, what of it? Isn't that a matter for them?

No. They're in error, and it's our duty to correct someone who is in error.

Well, I couldn't care less about that. What concerns me is

education. If we all had to go in with them, which is what they want, we'd have to have our children, or grandchildren in my case, taught in their schools, with all their beliefs. That's not on.

I can't see that. My brother and his family are in the South, and it just isn't an issue. In fact my daughter-in-law tells me they bend over backwards to provide Protestant schools, even when they're too small to be economic.

Do you think we might return to the text? 'There's no fear in love.' Does that have anything to do with this discussion?

It's a very hard saying.

Yes, and it becomes harder when we try to read it through the eyes of other people, but it's worth making the attempt.

I don't know if I can do that. I don't know enough about them.

That last comment was reminiscent of the white business man in Richmond, who said to the African American doctor, 'I was not allowed to see.' Although many Protestants, such as this Bible Study group, show a real reverence for Scripture, and a deeply felt sense of personal morality, they are apt to become very uncomfortable when discussion turns to the Roman Catholic Church, or their own neighbours: an air of unease descends, and they resort to stereotypical concerns, such as transubstantiation and indoctrination.

THE END OF PRIVILEGE

Politics provided a more lively forum, at a family Sunday lunch table.

Nicholas, you're interested in political matters, to judge by what you've written. I'd like you to try to understand something very significant. We [unionists] have always had high expectations; they've not always been realistic, but we've always had them, and they have been important to us. Take jobs, for example. Our people always felt they had a right to work. That matters, because a job's about more than the work. It's about looking after your family. It's about dignity, responsibility; and for many, it's about looking your friends in the eye at Lodge meetings. Jobs really matter.

That's right. When I was a wean, Harland and Wolfe had about twenty thousand workers. What is it now, about two thou? Maggie's to blame, you know. No subsidies. Stand on your own feet.

Liverpool Docks were like that, and the coal mines.

Yes, but here it was the same in other industries too: Gallaher's [tobacco] and the linen industry in Belfast and Londonderry. But they've all gone, those jobs, or most of them.

That's a mixture of technology and market forces. It should have been foreseen, because it's very dangerous. I'm told there are whole streets, whole blocks of flats in Belfast where nobody works – Protestant people, I'm talking about, and they've no hope of a job either, because they never needed qualifications.

That's it. A word in the right ear, who you knew, that's how it was done.

It's very helpful for me to hear this. Can I ask about the Roman Catholic community? Presumably they never knew the same security of employment – here in the North, I mean?

Well, no. That's right. But it doesn't seem to worry them the same way as it does us Prods. They never had work, most of them, and what you've never known, you never miss – not that I'm saying it's right, mind you. I've some very good Catholic friends, so I have. It's the emigration that's so frightening. All the best youngsters are going abroad to Britain.

Did you say abroad *to Britain?*

Well, you know what I mean! We can't afford to lose them.

They're our future. When they've lived somewhere else, they don't want to come back. My brother's kids have all gone off to college and university, all four of them. The parents were very upset, though they wanted to do the best for them, as we all would.

Well, I think they'll come back; they know which side their bread's buttered.

I don't think so, love. I don't think so, not when they've experienced the wider world.

I believe it's an even more serious problem among Protestant families in the Republic, especially in rural areas. I've been told about Protestant dances, where minibuses of kids are taken to try to match them up with good Protestant stock and encourage them to stay. A farmer described it to me as 'a careful breeding programme.'

It still happens up here.

Well, mixed marriages would be preferable to that, right enough . . . New blood . . . It's easier these days, for the children and that.

I wonder whether we're not really talking about a sense of superiority? It's easy to joke about the lengths people go to preserve their own particular social or religious group, but underneath it is something rather unpleasant, wouldn't you say? I mean 'class'.

Yes, I'd have to say that's true. But there can't be anything wrong in trying to preserve the way you were brought up, educated. Anybody would want to defend their own. We have a very good life here, and we want to keep it.

Do you mind me saying, you've said 'we' again? There are a good many people in the six counties who'd be very hard-put to say something like that, and they're by no means all Catholic.

I was told a sad story when I was in Galway. An old man – Church of Ireland in the North – was brought down south to see his son and daughter-in-law – they're a mixed marriage. He took a lot of persuading, but the grandchildren were an added incentive. As I say, he was very old, and not too well. He had a wonderful week. The whole experience was a revelation to him. He said 'The people are so soft-spoken and friendly, and the country's beautiful. I wish I'd known sooner.' His son told me so many people here follow the TV adverts, and take their holidays in Spain or Majorca or wherever. They'd never even consider a holiday in the Republic.

You can understand that. It'd be a question of whether they could sleep soundly of a night, but it's a good story, all the same. It makes you think. There must be lots like that old boy. What happened to him, by the way?

He died soon afterwards. A geography lecturer in Northern Ireland told me Ulster is the centre of the universe for lots of people here – like the old maps which used to show England twice the size of Europe or America, only here it's the six counties.

I wouldn't argue with that. It's all we've got, and if you don't walk tall, they'll trample on you. You will come and see us again, won't you? It's been good to chat.

It had indeed been good to receive hospitality from that family. They were very truthful and positive, and not afraid to think rationally, though hints of fear and prejudice showed through. Such rationality, though, was not always my experience.

THEY'RE DIFFERENT, YOU KNOW

I met with some Presbyterians in Belfast, and talked about the ecumenical scene in Liverpool. I asked for their reaction to our close working relationships.

What you've got to understand is this. This island is awash with Catholics, and it's getting worse. The way they're going, we'll soon be swamped.

If that's the case, don't you think it might be better to try to begin establishing a relationship?

How could you? England's a Protestant country, and you're a

Protestant minister. I'd have thought you'd understand. They're different, you know. If you'd mixed with them, really mixed, you'd know.

As a matter of interest, how many Roman Catholics do you think there are in Protestant England?

Well, lots from the Free State, but there can't be many over-all.

More than in the whole island of Ireland, by a long way.

Can't be! God help you!

Well, it happens to be true, but it's not an issue. England is no longer a Protestant country as you are describing it; in fact, I'm afraid it's hard to describe it as Christian at all in any real sense. The days when good Bible-believing church-goers doffed their caps to the monarch as the Protestant Defender of a Protestant Faith are long gone.

Not here, they're not!

A little later I raised with the group the question which had often arisen about 'Irishness' and nationality. I asked them how they reacted to the suggestion that they had every right to call themselves Irish, as many of their Protestant forebears had done.

Doesn't really arise, nor will it. Whatever happens, we'll still be British.

Your Protestant ancestors wouldn't have seen it that way. In fact, they were proud of their Irishness. In the eighteenth and early nineteenth century, Catholics and Presbyterians were partners in adversity: both were persecuted by the Established Church. Protestants even raised money to help build Catholic churches in Belfast.

Wherever did you pick that up? Anyway, it was a long time ago.

What about Wolfe Tone? What about the United Irishmen? What I'm getting at is this: You've been here for centuries. OK, you were put here because it suited England at the time, but you've been here far longer than George Washington's earliest ancestors have been in

*America, and his descendants are proud to call themselves American.
And what about the Boers in South Africa? They define themselves
as Afrikaners – people of Africa – not Holland or Europe. I'm sorry
to go on like this, but I think it would be a wonderful thing if you
could discover common interests with the Roman Catholics. You could
help them to understand that it's a mistake, and a modern one, to
equate Irishness with Catholicism.*

They shook their heads, looked at each other, and made no
reply.

I had many conversations, too, with individuals in homes, shops
and bars. Many of the same themes constantly recurred in the
North, particularly the inherited suspicion of Roman
Catholicism. In the Republic, where the Protestant community is
now very small – perhaps as low as three per cent, it was much
less of an issue, and, indeed, a matter for wry comment.

Religion here in Dublin is honestly not an issue between us
and our friends. It's not something we'd normally discuss,
unless we happened to go to the same church. Mind you, we
got a bit of a shock once. We had a very senior cleric from the
North, a cathedral dignitary, staying with us, and we invited
some friends to dinner to meet him. He asked my wife,
'What are they?' When she began to describe their occupations, he said, 'No, I mean denominations.' We said it would
never occur to us to ask such a thing. He replied that it would
never occur to *him* to sit down with anyone unless he knew:
there might be Catholics present. We were quite shaken,
actually.

Another couple, a lecturer and his wife, moved south to take up
a post in Dublin. They bought a house. Friends from the North
telephoned and asked, 'What are the neighbours?' The same thing
happened.

One's a surveyor, the other's a teacher, and opposite
they're . . .

No, no. What religion?

Oh, they're all Roman Catholic, as you'd expect.

God! Who on earth do you talk to?

I stayed for several weeks in the Church of Ireland Theological College in Dublin. Although it is situated in the Republic, the majority of the students are from the North. The College Chaplain organizes, each year, a careful 'familiarization' programme, including tours of Dublin, and visits to other parts of the Republic. I asked one of the students how she reacted to moving down from the North.

> Frankly, I was very apprehensive. It sounds daft now, three years on, but my first thought was, 'I've never lived in the Third World before'. Having discovered what a beautiful city Dublin is – a modern, thriving European capital – I feel so stupid. And everybody has been so warm and welcoming. I suppose I inherited those opinions, but I guess they're still widely shared in our part of the world.

THE CURSE OF THE TROUBLES

When I went to east and west Belfast, which are, respectively, largely Protestant and Roman Catholic, it was not difficult to discover, without consciously seeking them, people who had been touched personally by 'the troubles'. East Belfast, around the Shankill Road, has the appearance of a tribal homeland. There are flags, more usually the red hand of Ulster than the union flag, and murals depicting historic victories over the Catholic enemy, or honouring present-day paramilitaries. I found it hard to remember I was in the United Kingdom, and the presence of armed police, and regular patrols by soldiers when I was there added to the sense of unreality.

> My dad was killed outside his house. They never caught the scum, but it had to be the provos, the dirty, murdering bastards. He'd been an RUC reservist, you see. He hadn't an enemy in the world, sure he hadn't, not one. He was a good, God-fearing man. I can't describe them that did it.

We were raised not to trust taigs [Catholics], and that's all there is about it. That's just the way it is round here. It's the same on their side. We keep ourselves to ourselves. It's better that way.

Do you have friends who are Catholic?

That's not the sort of question to ask here, Reverend.

My auntie was blown up by a bomb when she went shopping. What can you say about people who'd do that? You can't trust them, leastways my family never will.

I spent an hour in a bar with a community worker. On the surface it was friendly enough, but I felt all the time that I was being watched. A man came up, and looking me straight in the eyes, spoke to my companion:

Would your friend be a Fenian? [Catholic]

Not at all. He's a good Prod from Liverpool.

A little later, the same thing happened:

I don't believe we've seen your friend here before.

At this, I decided we should leave. I asked what would have happened if I had been a Catholic, and had admitted it. My friend said we'd have been asked to leave – fast.

Everybody said they wanted peace, but not at the price of their Britishness, and certainly not if it meant the Republic had any significant say in the affairs of the North.

I want peace. We all want peace. I'm fifty years old. I lost my father in the last war, so I know a bit about suffering. It can't go on for ever. I've no quarrel with Catholics as people, in fact some of us go in and out of each others' houses: there, that surprised you! But Ireland having a hand in Ulster, that wouldn't be right. It's *ours*.

I asked a young teacher how she found her work in east Belfast.

Underachievement, that's the curse. I've some very bright

children, but they'll never fulfil their potential, at least, very, very few of them. They've so little to look forward to here. The surroundings are so bad. They've no proper role-models, no incentives, and consequently they don't believe in themselves.

What about the paramilitaries?

That's the big unmentionable. If you ask me, they're recruiting on the quiet just now like there's no tomorrow.

What about culture and identity? I know about the bands and the parades and all that, but deeper things.

That's quite hard to say, you know, because the nationalists score hands down on culture: artists, writers, poets, musicians. That's all an important part of where they've come from. We have them too, but much more hidden. It's not part of the culture here, and that's a shame.

You've been very informative. Can I ask you one more question? I've heard a lot about the so-called bloodbath scenario: you know, take down the wall, remove the army, and wham, we'll drive the Catholics into the sea.

I'd not say this publicly, but I think that's crap. It never happened in Germany when the wall came down, and it doesn't look like happening in South Africa. I couldn't see it happening here.

It's an empty threat, then? There are a lot of guns floating around, by all accounts.

Maybe and maybe not, but that misses the point. There's very little to choose these days between the two communities in terms of deprivation, very little. They'd soon be fighting in a common cause. In fact, I wonder if that isn't beginning to dawn on the more perceptive unionists.

Such thoughtful analysis was not always forthcoming. One of my more bizarre encounters occurred in a town to the west of the province. I was on this occasion dressed in a clerical collar of the 'slip-in' variety, such as is often worn by Roman Catholic priests. I entered a café to have some lunch. I had noticed the red hand flag outside. I sat down and waited, and waited. The place was not busy. Eventually I signalled the waitress, who was dressed in the old-fashioned style of black dress and white apron.

Could you help me, please?

Only God can help you.

I told her I knew that, but would be glad of a menu. After a few more minutes, she duly returned with the said menu, sticking out of a Gideon Bible, which she slammed on the table in front of me. I am ashamed to say that I meekly told her I had lost my appetite, which was not true. I left to buy a sandwich from the newsagent, who had earlier greeted me most respectfully as 'Father'.

A DIFFERENT WORLD

I spent a very pleasant morning with a successful professional man, a Protestant, in a suburb of Dublin. He said a great deal which interested me very much. I was able to share with him much that others had told me. He was expansive in his comments:

> There is a curious ambivalence in the unionist community up north. Most of the working-class people belong to Orange Lodges. The Lodge exists (I think I'm quoting accurately) 'to cultivate brotherly kindness and charity, concord and unity'. That's not easy to reconcile with the marching season and support for paramilitaries, I can't deny that. But it's all about identity. For the Protestant people, the Battle of the Boyne was the defining event. Therein lies their security. It was a victory, a new beginning, something to be proud of, when the ancient foe was put to flight, all that sort of thing. Incidentally, there'll be no peace in this land until both communities feel secure in their own identity. Northern nationalists say we are the ones with the power. It no longer feels like that, and in east Belfast I doubt if it ever did. That's why unionists look back to a golden age.

I told my host of the prejudice I had encountered in the North, especially towards Catholics, and the fear that was so often evident in conversation.

Yes, there is fear, and I'd have to say that I share it, at least in part. The truth is, the Catholic Church in the Republic has had a real hold on many aspects of everyday life, like schools, healthcare, who you can and can't marry: really basic things. In a mature democracy, people should have the freedom to make up their own minds about such matters, don't you think? Certainly most of my colleagues and friends around here think so.

The fear arises because it's hard to imagine that the church would not try to impose its will and its practices and its values on the whole community in the event of a united Ireland.

But non-Catholic friends down here in the Republic tell me there is no such coercion: indeed, rather the reverse. Has that not been your experience?

Yes, it has. But you see, Protestants make up less than five per cent of the population here. We're not a threat. But a million of us would be a different matter.

I should have thought that would make it even less likely. As a matter of fact, a number of Roman Catholic clergy and religious have spoken to me about the terrific decline in Mass-going and their influence on the young. One said 'we're in real trouble'.

Well, that's probably true. We live in an increasingly secular age. But what worries me is that they go on about Vatican II, and how everything's changed: how ecumenical they are, and open. Do you seriously believe this Pope has the slightest interest in Vatican II? I hear he'd bury it tomorrow if he could. If you ask me, friendliness towards Protestants – and a lot of RCs are friendly – is because they'd like to absorb us . . . No, on reflection, I think that's going too far . . . But 'the one true church' is still alive, even though it's not kicking as hard these days; but you probably think I'm being a bit cynical, and I am!

I received an unexpected invitation, at this point, to stay for lunch. It gave me an opportunity to withdraw and write some notes on this non-stop flow of information, which continued on my return.

I'm prepared to say this to you on condition, and I mean it, that you give no hint whatsoever of my identity. I have the family to think of, even down here, but I respect what you're trying to do. I came down here [a few] years ago to get away from the all-pervasive security in the North. Parts of Belfast are like Eastern Europe as it used to be, perhaps worse. People in England have no idea. It's like a police-state.

Being here has given me space to think, read a bit. You know, I think we Protestants brought the troubles on ourselves. Pushing all the blame on the IRA is a classic case of scapegoating. For more than fifty years we had it all our own way. To hear my late parents talk, you'd have thought we lived in British India.

We offered the Catholics bugger-all (excuse my French). They needed to feel wanted – don't we all? Our leaders talked about loyalty, civilized Christian values and all the rest, and couldn't see they were doing the opposite. The English (no offence) talk about 'fair play, British justice, we're the most tolerant society on earth' and all that stuff, and allowed terrible things to go on in their own back-yard. That's why paramilitary violence has happened. It wasn't foisted on us from some Gulf state: it came from within, and it still draws its support from within. Not popular opinions, these, by the way.

But very honest ones. Thank you. Can I ask, with the objectivity you've found possible here, whether you see grounds for hope?

Yes. I think more and more thinking people are coming to see that there has to be change. The trouble is, they don't dare say it out loud: I'd be choosy where I spoke like this myself, by the way. I suppose you could say we've run out of the situation by coming down here.

Why did you settle here instead of Britain?

We've always lived in Ireland; so have generations of us, and we have a very good life and lovely friends; and it's a beautiful country, don't you think?

This is all so fascinating. Why don't you try and write something, and maybe send it to one of the papers in the North or in England – anonymously if you like? You're saying some very important things. Or perhaps you could try to persuade church leaders to open up discussion of these things in the North, as well as here.

One day, perhaps. Thanks for coming.

WE NEED A MIRACLE

I talked with a retired professional man in a Belfast suburb. He is a member of the Church of Ireland. He wanted to talk about the religious dimension of the conflict, and in particular the crucial role of the churches in England, especially the Church of England.

Canon, you are a priest in the Church of England. Your church holds the key to peace in Ireland. I have always believed that the National Church is the custodian of the soul of the nation. The behaviour of some bishops and archbishops does not always suggest their awareness of the fact, but I believe it.

Central to the church's task is the healing of the broken – broken-hearted and broken in body. The Protestants in this province are broken, wounded, disillusioned. Much of that is our own fault. But much is your fault. The government at Westminster, in playing around with the unionists because it needs their votes, is, after all, only doing what it's always done since it put them here.

The Protestant people of Ulster need help. They need a vision, whether that is of a strengthened union or of their proud potential within an all-Ireland Republic. They must have a vision. Instead, they are being made to shoulder the blame for being intransigent. 'We asked for bread and you gave us a stone.' This is at root a spiritual matter. Can you try to get the church in England to convince the powers-that-be of what's happening?

I'm proud of all that Britain has done in the world. Why is it that on this one issue of Ulster, it is so *dishonest*?

As you know, I have been suggesting that Britain should apologize to the peoples of this island, all of them, for the terrible things that have been said and done down the years, at least as a start.

Yes, friends sent us your piece; that's why we wanted to meet you. The danger is, it will be seen as one-sided, an apology to the Catholics only.

Yes, I see that, but I have never said so. In fact, I think increasingly that the Protestant people have been used, albeit differently.

And still are, and still are.

Have you any idea what form such an apology might take?

I think something along these lines: We have treated you very shabbily over the centuries. We have manipulated you and used you, and we are still doing so. That is very wrong, and we ask you to forgive us.

That's very honest. Who would offer such an apology?

I don't know. It would have to be a representative figure, perhaps Her Majesty the Queen. What I do know is that we need a miracle: a miracle of grace, like South Africa.

I was talking to a lady from South Africa the other week, curiously enough. She told me how Afrikaner friends had gathered in her house to watch the swearing-in of the new government. She told me many of them were in tears, and they were tears of joy. She said 'God has raised up two men of faith to do his will.' We should be praying that he'll do that in this divided land.

Amen to that.

THERE HAS BEEN A PROPHET AMONG THEM

After I had written this chapter, with all the comments from within the Protestant community, I took it to Dublin to discuss it with Senator Gordon Wilson, who was a constant source of encouragement to me. Gordon had become a deeply-admired figure after the death, at a Remembrance Day service in Enniskillen, of his daughter Marie. From his hospital bed he had disowned bitterness, and spoken of his Christian faith, and the need to forgive. The Queen made reference to Gordon in her next Christmas broadcast, and the Taoiseach, Albert Reynolds, invited him to sit in the Senate – the Upper House of the Irish Parliament.

I went to see him in Leinster House, in Dublin, between sittings. Gordon and Joan had just suffered further tragedy, in the death of their only son, Peter, in a car accident. Gordon spoke to me of his faith being tested to the limits. The certainty that they would all be reunited in heaven was the thing that most gave him strength to carry on. Typically, he then turned to my book.

He was particularly struck by the comments of the last man I had visited – the measured, reasonable and deeply Christian tone. He said those views were very much his own. He then asked how he could help me.

> *Could you possibly consider writing a foreword to my book, or perhaps a piece for the back cover?*

> Nicholas, if I can help you in any way, I will. I am honoured that you should have asked me, but, you know, I'm only a small-town draper. I doubt if anyone would want to read my poor words.

We agreed, in May 1995, that I would send him the manuscript in the autumn. Gordon Wilson died very suddenly a month after our meeting. In a powerful address in St Patrick's Cathedral, Dublin, on 2 July, Archbishop Donald Caird paid him this tribute:

> His contribution to reconciliation, to the healing of the psychological and spiritual wounds of centuries, has been incalculable. If anyone can be called a child of God for his efforts to make peace, the quiet business man from Enniskillen – the Senator and Justice of the Peace, Gordon Wilson – can . . . All who seek peace and reconciliation for our country remember him with pride and thanksgiving, and endorse the accolade –

'Well done, good and faithful servant' and know that 'there has been a prophet among us'.

Gordon must have the last word. In January 1995 he made a submission to the Forum for Peace and Reconciliation in Dublin. This is part of his contribution:

For too long, people in Northern Ireland have been shouting when they should have been talking, and talking when they should have been listening. If our hearts and attitudes are to soften, we must talk, and, above all, listen to one another. By listening carefully, each side can learn to trust the other's point of view, even if they cannot agree with it.

We can never agree on everything, but let us agree to differ in peace. Let us learn to find a new way to live together, based on the things we share, not least of which is the piece of earth we inhabit, and, above all, our common Maker.[2]

9 *A question of justice*

During 1993–94, I was able to meet and listen to nationalists and republicans from a wide range of backgrounds. I also encountered members of the Roman Catholic community who fall into neither of those categories, but who would prefer to see the retention of the union. I was able to meet people who live in west Belfast and Derry, and people in town and country who had been – or still are – active members of the republican movement. I also sought opinions in the Republic.

I have found these comments much more difficult to analyse than those of the unionists. For most Catholics in the North, the issue of British 'occupation' is a simple matter of justice denied; but an increasing number see themselves as materially better off under British rule than they would be in a united Ireland, ruled from Dublin. This attitude is a cause of serious resentment among the 'have-nots', many of whom feel they have been let down by their own people.

HELL WITH THE LID ON

If I had found east Belfast uncomfortable, the west was even more peculiar. People tended not to look at me. They were not at all rude, just strange. They seemed to look past me in shops, and there was an air of nervousness. I was not surprised. One could not fail to be aware of the ever-present security forces (in July 1994): fortified police stations, armoured cars, and, on the day I was there, following a nearby shooting, an all-intrusive helicopter overhead. I remarked to a local priest how strange it all felt to an outsider.

> Well, you see, we're being watched. The helicopter is filming everything and everybody. That's why people round here have a hunted look, or perhaps I should say haunted. They

know they're being watched, and, for all they know, listened to in their homes. There's no trust of strangers. When you've gone, you'll probably think to yourself, 'My God, that was like hell with the lid off.' Here it feels as though the lid is on, and very tightly on, at that.

What hope do you see? Does the Downing Street Declaration point to something new?

Hope, yes. We must have hope. I ask God to keep that alive, but that does not mean I'm optimistic.

A rather subtle distinction, Father?

Not at all. Hope is required of us; it's a Christian virtue. The other is a human emotion. I'm afraid it's a matter of experience.

What about schools? I've heard a bit about EMU (Education for Mutual Understanding). Is that beginning to make a difference, at least to children's attitudes?

Well, one of our teachers – a good lad – told me the weans have their own name for it: Education for Making Unionists! The pity of it is they can't see any future for themselves, not here.

I heard the same the other side of town.

I can believe it, but here they've known nothing different. They've nothing and nobody to look up to. You should meet one of our teachers: I'll arrange it.

What about the Church?

What about it?

Well, is it a helpful influence? Do most people here practise their Catholic faith?

Let's not confuse two things. Most people have faith, but faith in the Church is a different matter. I'd say most people know what the Hierarchy are after, and by and large they get it.

Forgive my ignorance. What's that?

Money. And influence with the government.

I met the young teacher the priest had mentioned. He confirmed much of what his opposite number in east Belfast had told me, especially about lack of hope and opportunity.

It's very hard to get through to the kids round here. I had a sixteen-year-old who wrote a very good essay about the troubles: original and perceptive. When I tried to praise him for it, he said 'Come off it! Why would you be saying that to *me*?' You see, they have no belief in their potential. That makes them very vulnerable to all sorts of influences, including violent ones. In some ways I guess it might almost be worse over east, because at least they've known better things once.

Not in recent memory on some of the estates, I hear.

Well, you could be fairly sure of some sort of a job. But here, you could weep for their future.

I was fortunate to meet an academic, who has made a particular study of Irish history from a nationalist standpoint.

The situation is terribly complex. I should think you hardly know if you're coming or going. We're talking about hidden undercurrents, private agendas. Nobody, and no group, is immune from some responsibility for where we are now. Politicians, for their own reasons, are reluctant to admit that, and the paramilitaries can't. The churches ought to be able to – they still have real influence – but they don't. It's sad. We are a Christian country with paralysed leadership.

Do you mean in church or politics?

I meant church, but it's true of both. My own Roman Catholic Church has a great deal to answer for. If you talk to the bishops, you'll find very little sign of regret, for example, for the catastrophic policy on mixed marriages, which caused so much pain and had a profound influence on emigration. Of course, the mixed-marriage issue wasn't really about carrying

on the faith − children being brought up good Catholics −
though that was what you were supposed to think.

What then?

Land. That's what it was about, and often still is. Everything
in this country is about land. Bring the next generation up as
Catholics and they'll inherit the land which was wrongfully
stolen from their ancestors. That's the point of the ban on
mixed marriages.

I've never heard that.

Well, it's not the sort of thing that would be openly admitted,
but that doesn't mean it's not true. Then take education. It's
the last power-base the Catholic Church has. There are
powerful arguments for denominational schools, actually, but
there must be parity of approach, genuine freedom of choice.

*Like local bishops allowing priests to prepare children for confirmation
in integrated schools, for example?*

You know about that one? Well, it's a not very subtle way of
saying the issue is not for discussion. Why should they be
afraid of freedom of choice? Actually, I think the message is
beginning to get through. Many middle-class parents are prepared to run the gauntlet of their local priest in favour of a
better education, or often the priest encourages them. That's
usually the way change happens.

The Presbyterians have their own difficulties, of course. A
good many of them still believe the Pope is the antichrist and
they are God's chosen people. Like the Jews, they have been
given the land. On that reckoning, we become the enemy,
the Philistines. Some of them, when they emigrated, behaved
the same way when they came across the American Indians,
by the way. It's the only way they know; it's deeply embed-
ded in their culture, and it makes them very insecure.

*Can I ask you what you think ought to happen now. I'm sorry if the
question is simplistic, but I'm struggling to come to grips with stuff
that seems so complex.*

It's the critical question. I'm not ducking it, but I'm going to put it in the form of a negative first.

I have become convinced beyond doubt that partition is not the best way to solve the Irish problem. That is my starting-point. The formula of the 1921 Treaty talks was never adequately met. It was agreed that all parties should meet to ascertain 'how the association of Ireland with the community of nations known as the British Empire can best be reconciled with Irish national aspirations'.

The Treaty and the Government of Ireland Act, most of which, by the way, has never been repealed, and still gives special privileges to Freemasons and Orangemen, have both failed.

The only long-term solution has to be a unitary state, because neither part of this island can survive economically by itself. Europe does its stuff in a big way, but what distorts the picture is Britain's colossal shoring-up of the North. Take that away, and a good many minds would rapidly be concentrated. I'm talking about 3.5 billion pounds a year, plus another 2.5 for security — all for six counties and one and a half million people. It makes no sense. How much longer are the British people going to wear that, when they look at the needs of their own cities and communities?

And take the army. I can remember the early days, when they used to describe themselves as impartial peace-keepers. You wouldn't hear that now, not after some of the things that have happened. If a peace-keeping force were still to be needed in the interim (and that's far from proven) it would have to be genuinely impartial, UN or Europe, but not forces of the nation which has the power. That's a classic imperial ploy.

So you're advocating a united Ireland with external guarantees. What about the Protestants? Can you seriously see them wearing that?

We come back to the pistol at the head argument. Look here, the political situation in the North of Ireland is dead and irrecoverable: fact. It must be undone: fact number two. The six county solution was never intended to be more than a short-term compromise. It's nonsensical. British yet not

British. Unionist yet separatist. Part of the UK, yet English parties don't organize here. It's a dead duck, and if it were Bosnia or some part of Africa it would be laughed out of court . . . but because it's Britain's oldest colony, you go on trying to enforce the unenforceable. To recognize that might just make a political solution possible. There's nothing new or original in all this, by the way. It's all old hat.

A WAR OF LIBERATION

With some of these ideas buzzing in my head, I decided to seek out a man who I knew had been an activist in the republican movement when he was younger. He was both imprisoned and interned without trial by the British. He took some finding in the heart of the countryside, but the journey was worthwhile. I visited him the day after a Chinook helicopter had crashed in Kintyre, killing the cream of Northern Ireland's anti-terrorist specialists. The images were on the television as I arrived.

You're welcome. Do you mind if I watch this for a moment?

What are your feelings as you look at that?

He paused for a long time before answering.

A lot of grieving families today.

After sharing food with me, he said:

Ireland is rather like South Africa, and the north east is the Transvaal. It's as if South Africa had decided on the solution of putting all the extreme right-wingers, the Terre-Blanches of this world, into the one territory – a sort of white homeland. If that's what they'd done, people would have said 'it can't last five minutes. It's a crazy solution', but that is more or less what was done here. It may look neat on paper, but it's crazy.

What you've got to understand is that it's a question of justice. There's so much nonsense talked about the IRA and primary violence. It is the illegal British presence in this land, in defiance of the wishes of the people of Ireland in 1918 that is the injustice.

Hence the armed struggle?

Hence the armed struggle. We have no quarrel with the Protestants as people, none at all; in fact I respect their religion. But if they identify themselves with the British state, wear British uniforms, serve the British government, then they know they run the risk of being eliminated. It's a war of liberation, and it makes me sick that there are even Catholic people here who can't see it.

Normal politics have not worked here. They didn't work under Stormont, and they've not worked since. We have been oppressed by your soldiers and your police. It's not us that have made it an armed struggle.

And the IRA?

Well, the Volunteers re-formed because of blunders by your people and brutality – there's no other word for it – by your soldiers.

Can I ask what you think of the Downing Street Declaration, which the two Governments have issued?

Well, it's an attempt. Actually, I think Mayhew is sincere; he's wrong, mind you, but he has tried, which is more than can be said for most of them. The whole process is misguided, because instead of putting British rule on the table for discussion, it assumes it's going to stay. It glosses over it with talk of power-sharing and all that, but as soon as you say it's for the people of the North to decide what happens, it gives the unionists a veto. That's not justice. I repeat, the Brits occupied the north of this land illegally. That's what they should be talking about.

The Protestants would argue that they've been here a very long time.

As I said, we've no quarrel with the Prods; they'll be welcome to stay. In fact we'll need them. But that border was drawn on a map for one reason only, to make sure of a Protestant majority for ever and a day. That's outrageous.

So the peace process is dead?

I never said that, but unless there's honesty, it'll be a stitch-up.

Would you support a cease-fire if it brought Sinn Féin to the table?

I might . . . but it couldn't be permanent unless things are changed permanently — what I've been saying. But I'm not confident. How can I be? Britain's not going to admit it's been wrong all this time. You only have to look at Thatcher and the hunger strikers. Let them die and then give in to their demands. My God!

Forgive me if I'm a bit slow, but as I understand it, the logic of what you are saying is that the only long-term solution is a united Ireland, by whatever means. Am I right? And if so, can you see the unionists agreeing to that? It doesn't add up, does it?

It would if they believed it was in their best interests.

But — I'm sorry to labour the point, but it's vital — can you really see that happening?

Why don't you think it could?

Well, I'm an outsider, but what I'm hearing is . . . well, for a start, the unionists are very fearful: they're afraid for their identity, and they're afraid of the Catholic Church. And then it seems to me that an increasing number of Catholics, mainly middle-class, but not only, want things to stay as they are. They're better off with the British. I know that's resented, but it's a fact of life that when people have bettered themselves, they want to turn their backs on the ghetto: it's happened among blacks in the States, and it's happening in cities in Britain. Add to that the real fear of the Northern Protestants which people feel in the Republic, and it's hard to see any mandate for change, isn't it?

Well, you've said a lot of things there. Are you saying most people want to keep partition?

That's what I've been hearing.

I don't believe you're right, unless Britain keeps on with the huge subsidies and the troops, which I don't believe your people will wear for much longer, and why should they?

*Well, let me put a hypothetical question. The new discussion docu-
ment provides for a referendum, or perhaps parallel ones North and
South, on the border issue. Just suppose what I say (and it's only
what I've picked up) is right: sixty, perhaps seventy per cent in favour
of the status quo. What then becomes of your armed struggle?
Where's the moral legitimacy you claim?*

It would be very sad. Some would say we'd have to accept it,
but I'm afraid that could not work. The answer to your question is that we'd have to go on fighting.

In defiance of democracy?

Look. As I said, it's a question of justice. Surely you can see
that: it's in the Bible, after all. As long as one British official
has jurisdiction over any part of this island because of the old
stitch-up, it is a moral duty to fight.

And democracy?

How *could* such a referendum be democratic? And besides –
this is the point you should latch on to – justice is more
important than democracy.

I left that house with very mixed feelings: depression at the
scenario of endless violence which was being suggested, but also
real respect for that man's honesty and thoughtfulness, and his
genuine respect for the Protestant community, his recognition of
Ireland's need of them.

IT'S A BRITISH PROBLEM.

I went next to 'Derry-stroke-Londonderry'. Even the army uses
the older, shorter form of the name, though while I was there, the
Unionist Party boycotted the opening ceremony of the new airport because the name had been changed from Eglinton to Derry
City. The town has become widely known as 'Stroke City'!
The centre of the city has been transformed in recent years by
an energetic and successful campaign to draw in grants for urban
regeneration, and the results are very impressive. But real tensions

exist. I visited a Protestant family in the Waterside district – across the River Foyle from the city itself – and they told me they had felt driven out.

> All round here are Protestants who used to live in the city. It's become impossible. The Catholics have collared all the money, and there's fewer and fewer of us left there now. It'll be solidly republican in a few years.

I asked nationalist community leaders about this.

> It's not true and it's not necessary. The unionists have tried to introduce a climate of fear in the Prod community, and they've been leaving, but most of us would regret that, in spite of the discrimination our people have suffered down the years.

On that, I've heard varied opinions on the position now with regard to discrimination, in housing, employment etc.

I expect you've heard it's all a thing of the past?

From some quarters, yes, I have.

Well, I wish it was. Discrimination did not end with Stormont. You get well-off, middle-class Catholics wanting to believe it, so they say it, and of course the NIO [Northern Ireland Office]. They've tried, I'll give them that, but the animosity is too deep.

Where?

In the Lodge. It's built-in.

Orange Lodge, you mean?

And the Masons. They've got the real power because they're a secret society. It's 'jobs for the boys'. That's why lodges exist, after all, to look after their own. And the Unionist Party's so riddled with the same that there can't be real progress, no matter what the government says. You must have heard them talk about 'a Protestant parliament for a Protestant people'. That means the rest can get lost.

This is the truth I'm giving you, right? Catholics now, in 1994, are two and a half times more likely to be out of work in the North of Ireland than Protestants. That's an official statistic, and if they *have* got jobs – Catholics, I mean – it's almost impossible to get promotion. I'll give you all the figures: I'm not making this up.

That was what sparked off the civil rights marches in the late sixties, wasn't it?

Right, and they were non-violent until the RUC pitched in, and then sent for the army.

They were about civil rights, then, and not a united Ireland.

Sure they were. United Ireland never came into it. We wanted fair and equal treatment, just as we'd have got in Britain. It was a question of justice. But now . . . well, now you've got something different again. They're so disillusioned that even equality's not going to be enough. They've lost trust, the ordinary Catholic people. Too much has happened.

What now, then?

Well, our problems are historical, right? Our people were treated like dirt by the Protestant settlers – I'm not even blaming them – they had to live too. But the point is, we lost our homes and our land and our livelihood, such as it was. It doesn't matter that it was a long time ago. It's never been put right. This century they've only made it worse, really put the boot in. There's no hope of dignity and respect if you've no job and no decent home.

What about the unionists if a united Ireland were to happen?

Not if – when. It's as certain as night follows day, but I doubt if I shall live to see it. Let's go and call on a friend of mine. He'll tell you some more. I don't want you to go away thinking I'm just a fanatic or something.

My host was as good as his word, and in fact managed to gather three of his friends for a further discussion.

Joe, the Canon was asking about a united Ireland, what would happen?

I was thinking of the position of the unionists. There are a lot of them.

Sure. They're entitled to their homes and their land. They've worked for them, many of them. They can stay. They can be equal. They can practise their religion and they can be good neighbours. All that is only fair: two wrongs have never made a right. But what they can't do is dictate to the State of Ireland its political future, and they can't blackmail Dublin over the constitution. That means no veto. They're an artificially created majority.

If you were the government, say the Secretary of State . . .?

Well, I'd be trying to persuade the unionists that it's in their own best interests to join a united Ireland. They're neither fish nor fowl as things stand. They don't belong to Britain – not really – and they won't belong to Ireland. They're out on a limb. The trouble with the latest initiative is that it's so negative. All this 'We have no interest in staying' stuff. Why not 'We believe it is in your interest to support a united Ireland'?

By such and such a date?

Exactly. We'll go on paying for a few years and then you're on your own.

And the army?

Could go tomorrow. Nothing would happen, because everybody would see they'd all be the losers.

There I can't agree, Brendan. There's too many guns. We'd need somebody to keep them apart.

The real trouble is, nobody but nobody even dares talk about a united Ireland – what it might mean, how it would work, what it would cost; can we get money from Europe and America: these are the things that matter. All we hear about is 'the Irish problem'. It's *not* an Irish problem, it's a British problem, because they started it, and they've got the power.

I've been welcomed in a very friendly way by almost everybody, Catholic, Protestant, you name it. From what you've been saying, I'd have thought you'd hate the sight of us.

No, no. There's no animosity towards English people, none at all. Your government's a different matter, but not the people. They are good people. After all, thousands of Irish are living alongside them in Britain, taking a full part in life there. That's the way it would be here.

People in Derry were more willing to talk, all in a highly articulate way, than in any other place I visited. I called on a family in the Bogside – the area which had been most involved in the early civil rights marches. There is still a huge sign on a gable-end: 'You are now entering Free Derry.' We talked about a sense of community, and the importance of community celebrations.

I'm all for a bit of celebration myself. It livens things up. We used to quite enjoy seeing the Prods march; you know, the music, it was all a bit of a game. And even the red, white and blue kerbstones, well, it did no harm at all.

You're using the past tense.

Well, it's not a game any more. It's got an edge to it now that it didn't have when we were younger. It's one in the eye to us now.

It's like they were fighting the battles all over again.

And defeating the Catholics?

Aye, defeat us, that's what they want.

And that hurts?

Of course it bloody hurts!

Many people tell me you'd be worse off, financially I mean, in a united Ireland. What do you feel about that?

I remember seeing Nelson Mandela – I think it was him, or it may have been another ANC fellow – it was a couple of years ago. Anyway, he said 'We'd rather be poor and have our freedom than poor and under the boot of an oppressor.' I never forgot it. Their principles were so strong, you know. I'd feel the same way.

Well, an awful lot wouldn't. Materialism reigns these days. When you've got it, you don't want to give it up.

Maybe they'll have to. We'll see. It'll not be long, anyway.

There was a photograph of a boy in a black-bordered frame on the mantelpiece. I asked if it was a relative.

Yes, it is. My nephew was murdered by the Paras on Bloody Sunday.[1]

As I was leaving, the same man, in whose house we had been talking, turned to me and said:

You know, Canon, there's only one thing rarer than spring flowers in the Bogside, and that's a listening Englishman.

WE LOOK TO OUR CHURCHES

I have tried to understand something of the curious position of the churches in all this. I had one – for me – very moving conversation with a Roman Catholic layman, whose disillusionment, not only with his own church, has become a matter of real pain.

It's important you take a long, hard look at the churches, because they are the key. They are not really interested in what Jesus taught any more. They think it's more important to stop people using condoms, and to keep people trapped in loveless marriages. That hurts, because we look to our churches for more than that.
    I'm not well-informed on church history and doctrine and those sorts of things, but the way I see it is like this. If you look at the Bible, it's hard to find things Christians can disagree about, really disagree, I mean. Take love, compassion,

healing, forgiveness, valuing people, what I call social love: caring for another human being as you would care about your own. That's basic, isn't it?

Here you've got three big power-bases: politics, education and church. None of them's working properly but the one that ought to be helping and strengthening the others – i.e. the church – is no less corrupt than the other two. Why? Power, that's why. They will not let go of power, and so they can't be any help.

I've heard a lot of people talking about identity, how each side needs to hold on to its own identity, which I suppose has to do with culture, customs, history. What do you think about that?

Well, it's basic to human nature, isn't it? We all need to discover our identity, our roots. That's why flags and music matter so much to people. The struggle for civil rights in other countries is very significant. It began in America, but South Africa and other black-African nations have taken it up. Oppressed peoples find a point of focus in their blackness. 'Black is beautiful' began as a slogan; it's become a reality for millions. It's the one thing that unites them, and it's a matter for pride, and it gives them power.

Here it's around Irishness. What does it mean to be Irish? There isn't really a memory of it, it has to be shaped. But if you ignore it or try to suppress it, boy, you've got trouble. But doesn't history show that, the world over?

What frightens me, really frightens, I mean, is all the anger, especially in the young people. It's got to go somewhere, and the paramilitaries are scooping them up in droves. You can't prevent it. Now that spells big, big trouble.

NO CRED. AT ALL

I caught the flavour of some of that anger in a bar in west Belfast, where I had been taken. It began badly, when I was asked:

What did you think of the helicopter crash?

I think it was horrible, especially for the families.

Aye. It was a shame, right enough. It was only half full.

A few Guinnesses later, reason prevailed, and this observation was made:

I am an Irish citizen, right? But I live in the North of Ireland, right? Now, I can't vote for Major, because the British parties don't operate over here. I can't vote for Reynolds [then the Irish Taoiseach] because it's against the law for me to vote in the twenty-six counties. I'm not saying I would vote for them, but you see what I'm getting at? Who is deciding my future? Those two. That's why the peace process has no cred. at all. We've got no part in it, and to make matters worse, the Prods can veto it if they don't like it. It's not fair.

I found much of this kind of anger in people of republican or nationalist sympathies, especially in less affluent areas. I had heard much talk, especially in west Belfast and Derry, about Catholics who have 'done well for themselves' and want to preserve their new-found way of life. Sitting on a well-cut lawn on a sunny day in a Belfast suburb, with a large gin and tonic in hand, it is very easy to be seduced.

People have switched off from politics, you know. They don't really care any more.

I don't think you'd find many people agreeing with you in the Falls or Ballymurphy.

I can see you've been listening to the hotheads, Canon. Nothing would ever satisfy them. You can't turn the clock back. That's the real point. There were bad times, terrible times, we've all known them. Yes, things were loaded against us, and nobody can justify the way the unionists in Stormont behaved, but things have moved on. The trouble could have been avoided if they brought in direct rule at the same time as the army, but, as I say, that's in the past.

You've got a lovely home here. You've done – please don't think me rude – very well for yourselves. How do you feel about your fellow

Catholics who have not 'made it'?

Every society has its winners and losers. It's easier to be a winner in Northern Ireland than in the Republic, and that goes for the poorer elements as well.

That was a far as I got, apart from an excellent lunch.

JUST LIKE MY MUM

I had two curious and revealing experiences at road-blocks. These, whether mounted by the army or the police, were a common feature of life in Northern Ireland, at least until the cease-fires. At one, in my clerical collar, I was stopped in south Armagh by an RUC patrol. A very young-looking policeman with a machine-gun, backed up by others, said:

You're not from these parts then, Father?

You must have noticed the English number-plate.

No, it wasn't that, sir. You smiled at us. That's kind of unusual around here.

In the second incident I was the passenger in a car driven by a Roman Catholic woman, an old friend. This time it was a young soldier, who asked her:

See your I.D. please, love?

Sorry, I haven't got it on me, but [pointing to the interior mirror] that's a very good likeness of me.

The soldier called his mate across.

We've got a right one here, Dave.

The second soldier looked at her, and said:

God, you look just like my mum.

We're on different sides, you know, sonny.

Yes, that's what's so effing stupid. On your way.

10 *A matter of religion?*

Ireland is a Christian country.[1] In the North, at least eighty per cent of the people claim Christian allegiance, and, although these days far fewer regularly attend a place of worship, people consciously think of themselves as Christian.

Terms such as 'Catholic' and 'Protestant' usually describe where people live, where they went to school. The one is unlikely to have much contact with the other: indeed, the 'other' is a cause of anxiety, and is usually defined, not as a separate denomination but as a different religion.

In Ireland – North and South – the local churches have a very important social function. This is especially true in rural areas, where life revolves around the local church community, from crèche to senior citizens' club. Most people are 'closed' to the other community except, perhaps, for individual friendships. The weight of history is a heavy one, and in many Presbyterian churches, the prevailing opinion would be that Roman Catholics are not Christian at all. That, indeed, would have been the general opinion in Liverpool in the recent past, not excluding a substantial section of the Church of England.

Churchpeople in Northern Ireland are touchy at the suggestion that it is Christians who are fighting one another. However, religion and identity, religion and culture, religion and politics are so closely intertwined there that it is impossible to say that the conflict is not a religious one. That being the case, any suggestion of a solution to the conflict must take into account the religious dimension.

One of the most alarming aspects of the present situation is precisely the reluctance of the churches to examine the religious issues. I would have to say, having met people at all levels of Church life in the North and in the Republic, including many in positions of leadership, that all the main denominations have a tendency to be conservative, cautious and defensive.

In Liverpool, I have experienced, and been the recipient of, real pressure from the laity for ecumenical dialogue and for teaching. In Northern Ireland, with isolated exceptions and in non-denominational centres such as Corymeela, Glencree and the Irish School of Ecumenics, ecumenical dialogue seems to be largely confined to church leaders, and even then, some Presbyterian moderators have declined to be involved. At a local level, occasions such as the annual Week of Prayer for Christian Unity tend to be well supported by Roman Catholics, who may wish to get to know their Protestant neighbours. That very fact makes such events a threat to Protestants, who stay away. The largest Protestant denomination in the North, the Presbyterian Church in Ireland, is determinedly non-ecumenical. It is not affiliated to the World Council of Churches or to the Council of Churches in Britain and Ireland.

WE'RE SELF-SUFFICIENT OVER HERE

It was put to me by a Presbyterian minister that the churches in Northern Ireland are the prisoners of their own success:

> We are self-sufficient over here. We have, in the main, very large attendances. Our people are generous. They look to their church for their social as well as their spiritual needs. Although I believe the decline in attendance by the Catholics is much more serious than ours, the same thing applies to them. Ecumenism is just not on the agenda, principally because we do not see the need of it. As for inter-faith, that's a complete non-starter. The new RE syllabus in the North was agreed by the four main churches – that was a significant step, by the way – but it is absolutely and exclusively Christian.

The churches have a distinguished record of pastoral care – as one Church of Ireland bishop put it, 'We are good at being chaplains to our own people.' What is less easy to discern is a prophetic stance, a Christian vision for the whole of society. That is not to say that there have not been prophetic voices: there certainly have been brave denunciations of violence, for example; but these have tended to be individual, and to dwell upon the fact of violence, rather than questioning its causes.

This tendency to stand back from taking risks is not easy to understand from outside, but it was put to me from a very senior source: 'You don't understand the pressure people put us under here.' This might, I was told, take the form of church members saying they will leave 'in droves', but might also have a more sinister aspect. Veiled threats and insinuations, involving the family, are not unknown. I asked,

> *Surely you are not referring to church leaders and their families being threatened?*

That is exactly what I am referring to.

> *But who would make such threats?*

I told you, members of the church. There are some very frightened people out there.

Whatever may be the significance of such insinuations, a Christian academic told me:

> Archbishops, bishops, moderators, district chairmen, you name them, they all make brave-sounding judgements. They condemn violence, they plead for calm at times of crisis, but most of the time they will not try to understand the underlying problems, the hurts, the grievances. And because the leadership won't ask the hard questions, their people won't, either.
>
> We are talking, you know, about something very fundamental. What I want my bishop – I'm an RC, but the same applies wherever – what I want him to do is point out that there is a difference between following Jesus and being a nationalist. In the case of Paisley and his followers, there's no such problem. He says he's 'for God and Ulster', so presumably he can't tell the difference, but I can. We're none of us, bishops, priests, ordinary mortals, half critical enough of ourselves and our churches.

I put this to another man, whose work is concerned with peace and reconciliation. He told me:

> There have been some very courageous moves. It's hard to be a Christian leader here, looking over your shoulder all the time, but there have been occasions when they have really helped. I remember the Declaration of Faith in 1986, issued by all four: RC, C of I, Methodist, Presbyterian. They really did spell out the dangers of false loyalty. It was an important moment.

> *And now?*

> Well, they try, and they agonize: believe me, how they agonize! And they pray, I know that. But they're tired. We're *all* tired here . . . sick and tired.

Douglas Johnson and Cynthia Sampson have commented on the stance of church leaders:

> Although institutional church leaders meet, issue statements against violence, and urge prayers for peace, many of these same leaders are criticized for resisting peace initiatives that might alter their own institutions, such as the formation of ecumenical bodies involving both Catholics and Protestants, integrated schooling, or mixed housing.[2]

I sought the advice of someone who has worked in the ecumenical scene for many years.

> *Can you help me, as an English Anglican, to make some sense of what I've been hearing. I've heard many good and charitable things said about the churches and their leaders. I've heard about particular reconciliation projects, like Corymeela, Rostrevor, Glencree, Columbanus, PACE, the Irish School of Ecumenics in Dublin, Glenstal Abbey,[3] and others I've forgotten. Good stories, all of them. But at the same time I'm picking up an undercurrent of criticism, mostly from within the churches, and a sense of frustration.*

> Well, the churches have become domesticated, that's the reason for the frustration. They do a first-class job looking after their own, but there's very little enthusiasm for mission or

looking beyond their own fold. In a sense, they reason, why should they? Most of them are still doing very nicely, thank you. Why rock the boat? The religious divide is at the heart of the conflict in the North, so I'm glad you're not ignoring the churches, but it's terribly complex.

I find it very hard to understand the fear of ecumenism, particularly among the nonconformists. It's so different in Liverpool.

There you have it. It is very different in Britain, and that has to be understood. Ecumenism is regarded with great suspicion. People will tell you either that it's a sell-out to Rome or compromising the central tenets of the faith. What they're really saying is that they live in a land – the North, I mean – where there is religious and cultural apartheid. That's the truth of the matter.

The Catholics have developed through the centuries a coercion mentality: always dominated, always oppressed. The Protestants have developed a siege mentality: no surrender, not an inch. Now then, each of those mind-sets is like a prison. Not only does it prevent any real ecumenical dialogue now, but it stops them getting in touch with each others' history and memories. That's a tragedy, because, if they did, they'd soon find their stories are dependent on each other. They would find there is so much they could rejoice in together.

Yes, I've found in Liverpool that story is enormously powerful, and when we've been able to share them, even though they're very different, we've become much less afraid of each other, and each other's beliefs.

Exactly. The ecumenical process is not the road to destruction; it leads to the Holy City, but how to convince people?

As you know, I've been trying to urge sorrow and penitence on people in Britain, as the only way to reconciliation.

Yes, but be very careful. Repentance is never straightforward. Dietrich Bonhoeffer warned of the perils of cheap grace, and forgiveness without repentance. It has to involve all parties, beginning with those who have the power. You've an uphill task persuading certain leaders over here. They're full of fear.

Church or State?

Oh, both, Nicholas, both.

I understand more fully the truth of the statement by Johnston and Sampson that: 'The churches, like their congregations, have become captives of their own traditions and thus over-identified with a single culture. A degree of distancing may therefore be required if they are to effectively serve both cultures in a reconciling capacity.'[4]

I tried to understand some of the feelings and perceptions of members of the main denominations – leaders, clergy, laity, who spoke to me.

THE CHURCH OF IRELAND

We have a king-sized identity crisis, if you really want to know. History has set us against the Romans. We have most doctrines in common, to be frank – the early ARCIC meetings showed that (Anglican and Roman Catholic International Commission). Yet there is this awful sense that if *they* believe it, we can't! I know it's barmy, but there you are. We're stuck in a kind of nostalgic time-warp. History has not been kind to the Church of Ireland ascendancy, and you can see why. We have always thought we're superior, that's the trouble, and we can't shed it, not even in the South, where our numbers are piffling.

A lot of our people – I'm tempted to say most of them, but that's not fair – worship the great god nostalgia. That's why we're so good at looking after our own, and so reluctant to stray outside. It would be a good thing if we could wash a few more feet, especially Catholic ones, but I can't see it happening.

The real trouble is, we've allowed ourselves to become a

Protestant denomination. The Church of England is secure enough in its identity to declare itself as catholic and reformed, which it is, but so are we. You wouldn't think so, mind you: the Calvinist influence has been too strong here. The tragedy is, we could become a real bridge between the traditions, as you are, but it'll take a generation or two, if there are any of us left. My Catholic friends have a tremendous respect for the C of I. They look up to us for all sorts of reasons: freedom of conscience, married priests, involvement of lay people, all that sort of thing, but I sometimes wonder if we really live up to it all. We're so darned respectable and middle-class. I cast envious eyes at all the youngsters coming out of Mass on Sundays.

THE PRESBYTERIAN CHURCH

We are trapped by the Westminster Confession of Faith. Even though it's been modified a number of times, it's in the blood, including all sorts of nastiness about the Pope, Catholics not being Christians and the need to believe in a literal way every word of Scripture.

It may sound a bit archaic, but there are plenty of people just waiting for a breech in the dam, waiting for us to put a foot wrong. Then they'd claim they are the true heirs, and I mean heirs: there's a great deal of money and property tied up in the Church, you know.

What about the time when there was real dissent?

Yes, there was, certainly in the 1790s. We were persecuted just like the Catholics, and that brought people together. It's not mentioned much these days, for obvious reasons. It's been conveniently forgotten. I know people are very critical of our moderator, and some of his predecessors, for the stand they've taken about worshipping with Catholics, and that sort of thing, but they've really no option, you know. They only serve for a year, and they are beholden to their electors. They haven't got the security of bishops, but certain of them have been brave enough to make a mark, in spite of that.

THE ROMAN CATHOLIC CHURCH

I would love to think we could put right some of the terrible things we have done. They were not consciously or deliberately terrible, but the result of being so numerically dominant. The mixed-marriage issue is the one which is most often levelled at us, but the way we have tried to exert influence over the Republic's government comes a close second. It's not the same now, you know, but it'll take a long time to convince people of that, and I can't blame them.

The Catholic Church has never been very consultative; it's not in its nature. Until the Second Vatican Council, it was more or less official policy to ignore other Christian bodies, so we have to learn new ways. Personally, I think we've come a very long way in a short time. But Cardinal Tomas O'Fiaich said we are the largest church numerically, so we must be the greatest in generosity. That still has to filter through.

We are in the middle of a revolution. Lots of people don't like revolutions, especially the old boys in the Curia, but it's unstoppable. That's why the ecumenical wind has become a light breeze. But the best antidote to fear is the Holy Spirit. Remember Pope John, a safe old boy, they all thought, but God thought differently. I'm very optimistic indeed.

THEY HAVE TO LEARN TO LOVE

Less obviously optimistic, but painfully honest, was this comment on the churches in Northern Ireland. It was made by a respected community leader in Derry:

The churches here are the key, but they have to teach the rest of us. They don't seem to have learnt the relationship between Jesus Christ and here and now. If they are to reach us, they have to learn to love. Never mind the bloody stupid things. Where is the basic disagreement on the teachings of Christ? I can't find it. He was never concerned with the structures of religion or the state, or playing safe. He was concerned with trust and holiness, with personal growth, with love . . . and he was very angry when he met hypocrisy.

That man, and he is a good and compassionate man who loves his Lord and wants again to love his church, is probably representative of many more. He says that the churches are the key; in his view they do not have a good record, in Northern Ireland, in terms of ecumenism, or even in speaking generously about each other. I am not sure that in Britain, after some eighty-five years of what has come to be known as the Ecumenical Movement, we can feel very superior. That is why the Liverpool experience has been so liberating, for me and many others.

Of all the lines of enquiry I have tried to pursue, that of the churches has presented me with the most difficulties. It is, I suppose, a fact of life that in every land, the gulf between what the Church of God is called to be and the actual reality is very wide: it is, after all, a human as well as a divine institution. Yet in Ireland, and particularly in the North, I had a tremendous sense of the unrealized potential to effect change which the churches possess.

The Church is called to be a sign of God's Kingdom, which is characterized, so Jesus tells us, by justice and peace and righteousness. Yet in Northern Ireland, the churches wear badges of identity, which have to do with victims and victors, oppressed and oppressors, winners and losers. In an all-Ireland context, the roles are usually reversed, and less significant, but still present.

Both 'sides' can appeal to history and Scripture to justify their present actions. The Protestants can identify with the people of Israel, God's chosen people who were given their land and forced to defend it; the Catholics to the dark years of exile, and the longing for justice and recompense. The analogy bears further examination, for, just as Israel was denounced by the prophets for neglecting the poor and trampling on the alien, so in Northern Ireland the 'winners', having obtained the power, proceeded to abuse it.

What is difficult for the outsider to grasp is that politics and religion in the North are so closely interwoven. The unionists do not want to share power with the nationalists, the Protestants with the

Catholics, for fear that it will lead to a united Ireland. It is perceived that Britain would now like to find a way of disengaging, and the result is alienation. The Protestants want to be British, but deep down they know that they are not. Thus scapegoating takes place on a large scale: Catholic by Protestant and vice versa, South by North, class by class, North by Britain.

Religion in Northern Ireland has been successful, and important, in fostering a sense of identity and belonging in both communities. Those senses of identity are in some crisis, it is true, but they still matter. The trouble is, fear has made it very difficult for those communities to reflect, still less to project, the Christian values for which in theory they stand: love, salvation, redemption, hope of resurrection, God's new creation – in short, Kingdom values. There is little or no consciousness of 'the other'. What do they think, stand for, feel?

The only way such awareness can come is by listening to each others' stories, finding the points of commonality and intersection, and thereby discovering how to offer – and more importantly receive – repentance and forgiveness. Only by some such means can difference be discovered as a gift and not a threat. Terence McCaughey, a Presbyterian scholar, has written: 'The ecumenical movement itself is essentially a question of allowing that already existing, unbroken and undivided church to come to expression here and now.'[5]

There is a desperate need for the prophetic voice to be rediscovered, and heeded. As a bishop told me, 'Prophecy is the enemy of expediency. We need to ask God to send us prophets to lead us out of darkness.'

Ireland is to a great extent imprisoned by its history and its memories. Both need to be redeemed if reconciliation is to be real at all levels. The churches are best placed to confront history, for the actions of God down the ages, and the way human beings have responded to them, are the stuff of the Christian religion. It is by questioning the historical record, searching for signs of God's presence and activity, that the person of faith comes to a mature judgement about the events in question, and thereby finds ways of relating faith to daily living. The Easter event – what really happened and why it matters – is the most compelling example.

None of us can escape the consequences of our history. We have to live with them, but we can seek to understand it better, and thereby begin to heal personal and social memories. In Ireland, perhaps more than anywhere else, the churches must provide the resources of vision and hope, underpinned by Scripture, in order to help people to find a new way forward, a way in which the poor will no longer cry out for justice while the well-off cry for peace.

11 *Sorrow and penitence*

I have tried to explain and justify my real sense that Britain has been the cause of much of the agony experienced by the people of Ireland down the centuries. I was gratified, though not entirely surprised, to discover that most of the people who took the trouble to write to me – from England, Scotland, Wales and both parts of Ireland – share that judgement.

By means of letters, articles, sermons and speeches, I have tried to argue that there can be no hope of true and lasting reconciliation in Ireland unless there is real sorrow and full-hearted penitence. Although this is a theological proposition, I believe it is also true to the insights of human psychology.

The theological aspect is important. We have already seen that some eighty per cent of the people of Northern Ireland claim allegiance to a Christian church. The comparable figure in England is thirteen per cent. If so many people reckon to take seriously the insights of the Christian faith, it cannot be wrong to apply those same insights to the conflict, which is usually depicted, after all, as sectarian.

DELIVER US FROM EVIL

The Church has always recognized, and taken very seriously, the reality of evil in the world. It has also taught, on the basis of the teachings and the actions of Jesus Christ, that evil can be overcome with the help of God.

The Psalms and the Old Testament prophets have much to say on the subject. God exhorts his people to turn from their evil ways: 'Depart from me, all you workers of evil' . . . 'Cease to do evil and do good' . . . 'Turn everyone of you from your evil ways' . . . 'Do not devise evil in your hearts.'[1] The individual soul wrestles with the problem: 'Though I walk through death's dark vale, I will fear no evil' . . . 'Deliver me, O Lord, from evil doers' (Pss. 23; 59), and so on.

The New Testament takes up each of these themes, especially in the epistles of Paul and John; but for individual Christians, the most common, and perhaps the most challenging reference, occurs in the Lord's Prayer: 'Deliver us from evil' (Matt. 6.13; Luke 11.4). When people make this petition, just what are they asking? Are they seeking protection from evil things which may happen to them, that they may not become the victims of other people's evil deeds or impulses – in other words, that they might be spared suffering? Or are they asking God to protect them from the evil which is within themselves, the thoughts which they harbour, the deeds which they are apt, or want, to do? If evil is a two-sided coin, from which aspect do they most need to be delivered?

Or does the prayer have a more social than personal dimension? For example, it is plainly evil to kill someone with a gun. Is it any less evil to cause somebody to be killed by apathy or neglect? This deceptively simple petition in fact opens up some very complex issues. To be delivered from evil might not mean to be rescued from it, but to see it with fresh eyes and in a new light. Christians might well describe that as the light of Christ.

To consider evil in this social or corporate way is not by any means to be released from personal responsibility. Albert Speer, Hitler's minister for armament production, was the only Nazi minister to admit his guilt. His words are instructive:

> Things that would have shocked and horrified me in 1934, such as assassination of opposition leaders, the persecution of the Jews, the incarceration and torture of innocent men in concentration camps, I tolerated as unfortunate excesses in 1935; and things I couldn't have stomached in 1935 were palatable a few years later. This happened in one way or another to all of us in Germany. As the Nazi environment enveloped us, its evils grew invisible because we were part of them. If I was ignorant, I ensured my own ignorance. If I did not see, it was because I did not want to see.[2]

Evil is insidious. It enables people, by progressive steps, to regard other people as different, and therefore not their concern. From that point, it is a small matter to regard them as expendable.

The more I have reflected on the agony of Northern Ireland, the more I have found myself considering the subject of evil. I am at the same time forced to conclude that human beings' capacity to kill and commit atrocities is no more than an extension of the dark impulses which lurk inside me, if not in most of us. In my case they reveal themselves in relatively harmless ways: the effortless superiority with which I belittle people, or the exclusion of those who are 'different' from my circle of friends. Such attitudes enable me to rationalize, and thereby to exclude from my concern, the hungry, the homeless, or people of a different race or culture, just as Speer excluded the Jews, and many of my loyalist friends, by their own admission, exclude Roman Catholics.

If the petition about evil in the Lord's Prayer is offered in faith, the answer may not come as a relief. It may, on one level, turn the ones who pray from evil deeds, but on the other, it may lead them to recognize injustice, to feel others' pain, and to realize that social evil within our world is real and powerful and wrong.

Like so many of Jesus' sayings which, taken at face value seem so straightforward, this is in fact a very hard lesson indeed. I have discovered with interest some words of Barbara Taylor, an American Anglican priest. I have returned to them several times in the course of my Irish conversations.

> The real difficulty is not for sinners – their hearts are already broken – but the righteous. [They] are like vaults. They are so full of their precious values, and so defended against those who do not share them, that even the dynamite of the Gospel has little effect on them. 'Woe to you pharisees,' wails Jesus, 'for you tithe mint and rue and herbs of all kinds, and neglect justice and the love of God.'[3]

Jesus did not find it necessary to explain or define evil; still less did he seek to overcome it with evil: he knew that the old philosophy of 'an eye for an eye' would leave everyone blind. His way was to overcome evil with good. It did not, of course, prevent him from suffering; but in his suffering and death, his followers are given some idea of the resources with which they are to meet evil in their own lives and in society.

God's way, as demonstrated by Jesus, is always the way of sacrifice. For most of his followers, this will not mean the ultimate sacrifice of the cross, but lives dedicated to the service of those whom God regards as blessed: the peacemakers, the persecuted, the meek and the merciful, the pure in heart and the poor.

Christians pray the Lord's Prayer every time they go to church, and probably nearly every time they pray. If it could be prayed with understanding and real expectancy, then many might be led to understand that it is for them to accept their share of sacrifice: in their own way, and not only in their own circle, to overcome evil with good. That inevitably involves all who call themselves Christian facing up to the reality of evil in themselves and in the world.

In the Irish context, Bishop John Baker has some important things to say on the subject of evil. Writing of the fatal legacy which England has bequeathed to the people of Ireland, he says:

> Theologically it bears the distinguishing mark of true evil, namely that there is no right answer to the problems it poses. There is no rational step forward which is not open to fatal objections, not least because of the element of moral justification for the hard line taken by each side . . . The first thing to do about evil is to acknowledge its existence and its peculiar power. This step is itself creative.
>
> But acknowledging defeat is also, and more especially, creative for a community. Why? Because it creates fellowship, it binds together . . . The only thing that unites loyalists and republicans at a deep level, and equally unites with them the people of Great Britain, is our common failure, our inability to offer even a plausible answer to the misery of Northern Ireland. To accept this is, of course, something else as well, because it means admitting to each other that our own answers, bred out of our group history, are no good . . . Each of [the] main options is an invitation to disaster. The start must be to face this fact. In theology we call it the need for redemption, the fact that we cannot save ourselves.

Such a move is also an act of true penitence, because it means admitting that the behaviour of the other groups springs from desires that are not inherently wicked, and that by fighting for our own corner, we are frustrating these justifiable ambitions.[4]

THE SINS OF THE FATHERS

John Baker's words lead us back to sorrow and penitence. The reader who does not have a personal faith, or who has never given much thought to these matters, may find this concentration on such religious notions as evil and penitence curious, or at best irrelevant. But Ireland, in both its parts, is a deeply religious country. We in Britain would do well to recognize that dimension, and to examine the possibility that religious insights may provide a way – perhaps, indeed, the only way – forward.

It is a fact of life that violence breeds violence – blood will have blood. 'If Christians go along with this, however, if they acquiesce in such behaviour, they have forgotten their calling in a fallen world.' That is a harsh judgement. It was made by the Revd Douglas Powell, who died in Easter week 1994. Fr Powell was a distinguished Church historian, who had been my personal tutor at the University of Exeter in the late 1960s. He had made a study of penitence and penance, and gave me the benefit of his thinking, a few months before he died. He also said I might draw upon this material,[5] and I do so with profound gratitude for all that Douglas gave to me and to many students over a lifetime of academic rigour.

It is a fact of experience, as well as a saying from Scripture, that the sins of the fathers are visited upon the children for generations. We are ready enough to claim for ourselves the virtues of our parents and grandparents and their forebears; but could they really have been entirely virtuous?

Furthermore, nations behave in peacetime, but especially in war, on the basis that the end justifies the means. This philosophy has no doubt guided Britain in its dealings with Ireland and the Irish, from the twelfth century to the twentieth. How then can it be right to speak in terms of responsibility, still more of repentance?

Bloody events which lie in the past are not our fault; but the truth is, we cannot escape the legacy. History casts a malign cloud over present reality. Even though terrible things have been done in Ireland down the centuries, and certainly within our own, by both sides, one party has always to make the first move in expressing regret and making forgiveness possible. Divine forgiveness is unconditional; the human kind generally depends upon some expression of contrition. This inevitably involves risk: of ridicule, naiveté, pandering to terrorism, even lack of patriotism, yet it may be the only way in which a real breakthrough can occur. In a British-Irish context, what would be required would be an expression of sorrow and repentance for Britain's part in creating a horrible situation, and an appropriate, if not proportionate, penance. This would take the form of some practical reparation.

The concept of sin has gone out of fashion. Even the churches, in revising their services, have placed less weight on personal confession, and more on the joy of being united to one another in Christ. At the same time, society, especially through the popular media, has tended to become *more* censorious, especially about lapses in personal moral behaviour by public figures. Today, we are perhaps prone to regard ourselves as thoroughly moderate and reasonable: to say (or at least to think) 'If only other people were more like us.' Our Christian ancestors would have been more ready to recognize the truth: they are!

When we look at acts of cruelty and violence, and few of us can readily escape doing so, we find ourselves asking, 'How can they do it?' Yet if we look searchingly at our own nature, more deeply into ourselves, we shall discover a pool of violence, a well of anger, which seldom if ever finds public expression. A pleasant, mild-mannered family man, who loves children and animals, may in certain circumstances, such as war or an attack on those people or things he prizes most, behave in a way which seems quite out of character. He may do atrocious and cruel things. In those particular and unusual circumstances, it will have seemed quite natural.

There are not many sins that we condemn in others, the seeds of which are not inside us. If they have not borne fruit, openly at least, that may well be because of where providence, or accident of birth, has set us. As the observer of a public execution said, 'There but for the grace of God go I.' Recognition of this truth demands thanksgiving and humility, not righteous indignation.

The modern argument against what the Christian religion has traditionally called sin is, 'it doesn't do any harm.' But we are seldom the best judges of that, and even less likely to recognize that frustration and hurtfulness in others may well be due to our own arrogance or indifference. Or perhaps, if we are certain that we are never arrogant or indifferent, it is a question of our innate sense of our own superiority, our contemptuous avoidance of 'those sorts of people'. 'A person is known by the company he keeps,' we say. Douglas Powell dryly observed: 'Indeed. It was that which brought Jesus to the cross.'

If we throw a stone into a pond, the ripples spread long after the stone itself has gone. Sometimes they combine or conflict with ripples from other stones, and chaos results. The same is true of history. Upsets and upheavals are not usually caused by deliberate malice, but by people doing things which did not seem to do anyone any harm at the time. They simply seemed the natural thing to do.

Every act of sin has avoidable consequences. We may avoid them, but others will suffer for them. 'The sins of the fathers are visited upon the children unto the third and fourth generations,' and further. And our sins are visited on others, to the furthest limits of the oppressed and underdeveloped nations of the world. We affect others not only by what we do but by what we are. We create our public image by what we outwardly do, but it is by what we do inwardly, and what we think, that we make ourselves. And it is what we are that has the deepest effect on those we come into contact with. We help to make them what they are, and they affect others, and so the ripples spread, wider still and wider.

For Christians, it is not good enough to condemn the sins of the world as if we were detached from them. We are called to fix our eyes upon Christ on his cross – as the old Prayer Book describes him: 'The one full, perfect and sufficient sacrifice, oblation and satisfaction for the sins of the whole world.'[6] That is not just picturesque Tudor language, some piece of religious pedantry to fascinate professional theologians. It means that we are all sufficiently bound up in the sins of the world to need to repent for them.

Whenever Christ is crucified over again (and 'inasmuch as you did it to the least of these my brethren, you did it to me') we need to ask ourselves, are the perpetrators part of a web of seemingly innocent and self-seeking interests? And among those, do our own innocent-seeming and self-seeking interests have their part?

The fact of the matter is, our sins are among the sins of the world; but that is little comfort: indeed, it is the trouble. *All* have sinned and fallen short. That is why we need to repent for our own sins, not because they spoil our image or because we may suffer some comeback, but because they do harm to others. We may not see it, we do not intend it, but the people who are harmed are real people who, like us, have only one life to live.

A price must be paid for sin – it is penance. Penitence, or repentance, is a spiritual attitude: penance is an action. Repentance which does not lead to penance is likely to leave room for continuing self-justification. It is therefore not true Christian repentance. Penance is a vital part of penitence. If we can repent for the sins of the whole world, we can begin to accept hardship and injustice as penance for the sins of the whole world, of which ours are a significant part. We are bound to fail, of course – that is a fact of human nature – but repentance is a matter of hope, not despair, because we dare to believe that God does not despair of us.

CORPORATE PENITENCE

Now, this may all seem far removed from the main subject of this book, but I would argue, in the context of Britain and Ireland, that it is highly relevant. Political initiatives can take us so far, but the weight of history remains largely unaddressed. We cannot unlive it, but if we face it with courage, as Maya Angelou advocates, we may escape living it again. That will almost certainly be a painful process.

President Richard Von Weizsäcker of the Federal Republic of Germany made a highly important speech to the *Bundestag* on 8 May 1985, on the evils of the Nazi era.

No feeling person expects [young Germans now] to wear a hair shirt merely because they are Germans. Yet their forefathers have bequeathed them a heavy legacy . . . All of us, whether guilty or not, whether old or young, must accept the past.

Whoever closes his eyes to the past becomes blind to the present. Whoever does not wish to remember inhumanity becomes susceptible to the dangers of new infection.[7]

A similar theme was pursued by Lord Runcie, the former Archbishop of Canterbury, in his sermon at a service in May 1995, commemorating the fiftieth anniversary of the liberation of the Channel Islands from German occupation:

We cannot deny that in such circumstances as those of the occupation . . . there are painful and bitter memories: wounds within a community which still have to heal. [We all have] a duty to look back and consider carefully what happened. The lessons are not simple: we will have to work hard to look at the past and see its meaning: to look at a complete picture. We may even find that the meaning of the whole picture is not quite what we thought fifty years ago.

It is in understanding that healing comes. Those who do not wish to look at the past or understand the past or heal our memories are the sort of people who become easy victims of fatal lies and suspicions about other people in the present.

Sorrow and penitence are the Church's business, but they have a wider and more worldly relevance. They are valuable in their own right. The consequences of sincere sorrow and penitence are plain and visible, and beneficial to the circles within which the penitent moves. Above all, they provide a means, and sometimes the only means, to break an inherent pattern of evil, and to make possible new freedom of action.

But can theology – a religious proposition – be brought to bear upon the harsh world of politics? Clearly, as a priest, I would assert that it can and should; but is there a more objective justification for the politics of penitence?

An axiom of political life is always to be able to justify a decision, once made (though often without explaining it). If things go badly wrong, an apology is seldom forthcoming, for to apologize is to display weakness, whether offered for an insensitive or hurtful policy in the recent past, or as an attempt to atone for evils long ago. The point of an apology, however, even if pain is not healed by such a gesture, is that it provides a means of engendering good will. Gareth Steadman Jones has written:

> There is no reason in principle why . . . political and historical apologies should be considered absurd. Since 1945 some major political leaders and even one or two heads of state have made apologies for past actions for which they can only be considered symbolically responsible. But the effect has generally been positive.
>
> The main point about apologies is that the good they can bring about is mainly to the benefit of the perpetrator, not the victim. For the victim, the effects of an evil action are manifold: it affects not just one set of individuals, but their families, their descendants, their friends, neighbourhoods, regions and nations. The benefit that victims can receive derives not from the apology, but from the actions that substantiate that apology.[8]

Penitence, by its very nature, is a personal matter. It is pertinent to ask, then, can nations or communities remember, repent and forgive? In an important and timely book, Donald W. Shriver Jr argues persuasively that they can: 'Rare as it may be in politics, however, there is such a thing as the repentance of institutions.'[9] Shriver applies this theory to three twentieth-century issues which have shaped the lives of the American people: the United States and Germany; the official treatment of Japanese Americans during and after the Second World War; and the inequality experienced by African Americans.

The Japanese American question is a disturbing one. These citizens experienced internment, evacuation and widespread vilification during the Second World War. For decades they pressed for acts of public apology and symbolic restitution. Eventually their campaign bore fruit, and in a remarkable way. In February 1976 (the bi-centenary of the Declaration of Independence) President Gerald Ford made a proclamation which contained these words:

'An honest reckoning . . . must include a recognition of our national mistakes as well as our national achievements. Learning from our mistakes is not pleasant, but . . . we must do so if we want to avoid repeating them.[10] The President went on to speak of the treatment meted out to Japanese Americans '[who] were and are loyal Americans'. 'I call upon the American people to affirm with me this American Promise – that we have learned from the tragedy of that long-ago experience forever to treasure liberty and justice for each individual American, and resolve that this kind of action shall never again be repeated.'

Even that was not the end of the matter. Twelve years later, compensation payments were made to those still alive, and a foundation was established to promote Japanese-American cultural and historical concerns. Apology and reparation – penitence and penance – belonged together. President George Bush said: 'We can never fully right the wrongs of the past. But we can take a clear stand for justice and recognize that serious injustices were done to Japanese Americans during World War II.'[11]

Apology is always hard, but it is an essential prerequisite of true and lasting reconciliation, and infinitely worth the effort.

ON OUR KNEES BEFORE GOD

An international example with which people in Britain and Ireland may more readily identify is South Africa. Nelson Mandela has been recognized the world over as a statesman of outstanding courage and extraordinary magnanimity. His predecessor as State President has not received comparable attention. F. W. de Klerk's role in bringing about a multi-racial, democratic South Africa was scarcely less astonishing than Mandela's, and in one respect, perhaps, even more so. Like many of the unionists in Northern Ireland, de Klerk came from a deeply conservative and Protestant background. He was elected by his colleagues as leader of the National Party because he was perceived to have a safe pair of hands, and would be unlikely to cause trouble. Indeed, nothing in his background or career to date suggested otherwise. How wrong they were!

In the 1994 Nobel Laureate lecture in the Royal Albert Hall,

London, de Klerk told 3,000 people just how the new South Africa had come about, and he addressed the fears of those who predict that within ten years, South Africa will be the setting for yet another civil war, or will subside to the levels of corruption and inefficiency which characterize other African states. He concluded his lecture with these words:

> Despite the bitterness and divisions of the past, there is a growing realisation that none of us can prosper if we do not all prosper. I have faith in the integrity and commitment of leaders of the calibre of President Mandela and Dr Buthelezi. I have faith in the goodwill and good sense of my fellow South Africans. I have faith in our new constitution, and I have faith in God Almighty, in whose hands lies the destiny of nations.[12]

Those last words are deeply significant, for, a month earlier, in Cape Town, de Klerk had expressed deep apology to all the people of his country for the misery which apartheid had inflicted on his fellow-citizens: 'Deep regret goes much further than saying you are sorry. Deep regret says that if I could turn the clock back and if I could do anything about it, I would have wanted to have avoided it.'[13]

He went on to say that he and his party wished to break from that which was wrong in the past. He said it had never been their aim to deprive people of their rights, and cause misery, but separate development and apartheid had done just that. Even more startling and heartwarming was his response to a question from the floor of the Royal Albert Hall after his Nobel Laureate lecture. Asked whether it was international sanctions which had brought about the end of apartheid, de Klerk replied: 'It was not the sanctions, but deep self analysis on our knees before God.' At this point, a black South African in the audience said he never thought he would live to see such a day. He believed God had sent Mr de Klerk to his land.

Apartheid and the manifest injustices of the South African political system provide a clear-cut agenda for which sorrow and penitence might be expressed. Ireland is less straightforward, but the effects of the bitterness which festers in the hearts and minds of many Irish people for the way in which they and their island have been treated and used by Britain for generations, is an area ripe for the expression of deep regret. The hundred and fiftieth anniversary of the great famine has brought much of this to the surface, but that is one episode, albeit a great calamity, among many others over the centuries.

To apologize is not to demonstrate weakness. Rather, it requires a particular kind of courage and statesmanship which transcends politics. There will always be those who misunderstand or reject such gestures, but there are times when representative leadership – especially by a non-elected head of state – can speak of higher values. When the head of state is a monarch, who has a particular, if symbolic, role in relation to the National Church, an apology may be held to have spiritual as well as worldly significance. Others may choose to accept or reject such a gesture – that is a matter for them. The importance of the apology lies in the humility which it presupposes. There are times when politics alone is not enough.

12 *Towards a lasting peace*

It is said that there is no such thing as history. There are events, and people who choose to chronicle them bring to that task, consciously or unconsciously, their own presuppositions and prejudices. On any reading, however, the course of Irish history has been marked by suffering and tragedy on a scale unparalleled in any other Western European nation.

To be sure, there were in each generation cogent reasons for particular policies – there usually are. At different times, for example, there has been a real fear that Ireland would be used as a 'jumping-off point' into Britain by other nations, in particular France and Spain. The threat was not an idle one. Henry II feared his own barons, the enemy within; but James I had good reason to fear Spain; Cromwell feared those Royalist supporters who had fled to the continent; William Pitt feared the French; Asquith the Germans; and Churchill badly needed Northern ports as a lifeline in the struggle against Nazism and Fascism in the Second World War.

For these reasons, successive military forces were embarked and huge tracts of land were colonized, on which settlers were planted, whose loyalty to the British crown would not be in doubt. It is the conflict between those settlers and the native Irish, who were displaced, that has never been properly resolved.

A MORAL RESPONSIBILITY

Simplistic as many people find the notion, others firmly believe that Britain must be held principally responsible for all that followed. It was British actions that introduced artificial divisions to Ireland, most obviously by settling Protestant colonists into a Gaelic Catholic land. That historical and moral responsibility can now be seen, and ought to be properly acknowledged.

The Prime Minister declared in December 1993 that the British

Government no longer has any selfish strategic or economic interest in Northern Ireland.[1] This is a remarkable statement, and may have far-reaching implications for the future of the United Kingdom. As far as Ireland is concerned, it certainly reflects a new way of thinking, and no doubt owes much to the new economic and political reality in Europe, and the end of the Cold War. It may not be fanciful to suppose that it also reflects the hungry gaze of a hard-pressed Treasury, not least towards cuts in the armed services budget.

The truth is, at heart Britain would like to disengage from Northern Ireland; yet to announce its intention of doing so would be perceived to hand victory to terrorists, or to those who are believed to support them. Logic, however, points in the long term to such a course. Certainly my own conversations have suggested that a great many people in both parts of Ireland, whether or not they desire that end, expect a united Ireland to come to pass in the fullness of time. Reasons given include the apathy of most people in Britain, the colossal financial cost of maintaining the Union, the unsustainable military presence and the steady if unspectacular move towards Catholic numerical superiority in the North.

There are many who emphatically reject such an analysis, and who believe that the future lies in two states, one people. Among them is a distinguished churchman and former member of the Stormont cabinet, David Bleakley. In an important new book, *Peace in Ireland: Two States, One People*, he expresses the belief that the Downing Street Declaration and the subsequent Framework Documents provide a genuine breakthrough, a long-overdue recognition that 'ancient myths' about Britain and Ireland are at last being publicly questioned, and are giving way to 'modern realities'.

> Taken together, these assurances [in the Declaration] give room for creative expression of both traditions in Northern Ireland, and constitute a threat to neither. It also represents a final setting-aside of uncertainties and suspicions to do with outmoded colonial relationships. So, a new climate is created which uniquely challenges divisive notions of pan-Nationalism and pan-Unionism. Peacemakers look to the emergence of a

Pan-People's Front powered by the principles of the 1993 Declaration.[2]

Bleakley also advances the view that

North-South separation in citizenship is no longer seen as an insurmountable barrier to all-Irish progress. On the contrary, a proper use of what is on offer opens up attractive social and economic advances and provides a 'way into' real peace in Ireland. It is an idea whose time has come, and which is receiving island-wide endorsement.

So it is, among many deep-thinking people, and others who cannot bear the prospect of further violence; but there are also many for whom the deep pain of historic injustice provides an insuperable obstacle to 'two states, one people'. I gave Bleakley's book to nationalist friends in the North. They reacted with incredulity to the notion that the peace process presents no threat to nationalist aspirations. From where they stand, an effective unionist veto remains in place on any constitutional change. They regard the inbuilt unionist majority – to their way of thinking, an enforced majority – as an insuperable stumbling-block to long-term progress. They also criticize the language of the documents for implying that Northern Ireland's problems are to do with the political situation post-1969, and take little account of the deep historical roots of recent conflict.

SEEDS OF HOPE

John Major wrote of Northern Ireland, early in 1994: 'Dreadful deeds have been done by all sides in past centuries. We should regret that, but those of us alive today are not responsible for them.'[3] In an obvious sense, that statement is perfectly true. It does not, in its brevity, take account of the fact that none of us can escape the consequences of those regrettable deeds. I have elsewhere cited the examples of Germany and the Holocaust, Liverpool and the slave trade, and America and its internal conflicts. I have also suggested other international parallels, to which I have been able to add an extraordinarily generous apology, offered in August 1994 by President Herzog of Germany to the Polish people for the actions of the Nazi regime in Warsaw fifty years earlier. In the face of vociferous protests, notably from veterans, at the presence of German and Russian guests on Polish soil, President Lech Walesa nevertheless invited them, in a spirit of reconciliation. It showed moral leadership of a high order.

In each of these cases, in spite of the undeniable fact that terrible events are not the responsibility of 'those alive today', generous and unconditional attempts have been made to apologize, and thereby to open up the possibility of new beginnings.

In a little-reported but important speech in Coleraine in December 1992, the Secretary of State for Northern Ireland, Sir Patrick Mayhew, came close to a public acknowledgement of that need:

> The history of the island of Ireland as a whole, you will need no reminding, is in many respects both saddening and uplifting. You will not find me seeking to argue that Britain's role in Northern Ireland has only ever been associated with what has been uplifting. On the contrary, there is much in the long and often tragic history of Ireland for deep regret, and the British Government for its part shares that regret to the full.[4]

Colonialism, as one of my Irish correspondents indicated very graphically, leaves many problems in its wake. The violence which has become a part of daily life for many in Northern Ireland has cast its shadows over the Irish Republic, England, continental Europe, even Gibraltar. The truth is, we are all involved, whether we like it or not.

John Whale, in three 'Thoughts for the Day' on BBC Radio in July 1980, said of Northern Ireland:

> It is the beginning of wisdom to realize that we [i.e. the British] are responsible, historically and morally; we are both to blame and in charge. In any dilemma brought on by past moral failure, that is not a bad basis for a fresh approach – to be sorry, and to be open for the first time to other people's ideas.[5]

The Government of the Irish Republic has been fully involved in recent discussions towards a peaceful settlement. The United

States, where millions of people of Irish descent now live, has recently become more actively involved in the search for a solution. The European Community, within whose borders those of individual nation states are becoming less significant, also has a role. These external factors should be seen as opportunity and not as threat. In the same way, the decision of the IRA, followed by the loyalist paramilitaries, to discontinue the armed struggle, has opened up new opportunities for consultation on the way ahead. There are people in both communities in Northern Ireland who, whether from personal conviction or a deep sense that enough is enough, are beginning to dare to challenge stereotypes, to enter into dialogue, to examine all possibilities. Desperately fragile though the peace process is, there are seeds of hope.

INJUSTICE IN BOTH COMMUNITIES

Part of the reason for my choosing to spend a period of study-leave in Ireland was to test certain presuppositions and judgements. One such previous judgement has been abundantly confirmed. That is, the belief, which I have long held and expressed, that a great injustice has been done to the Catholic people of Ireland down the centuries. I am aware of the dangers of using terms like Catholic and Protestant, since those communities are not by any means monochrome in their political judgements, but here I believe the quasi-religious labels are accurately descriptive.

The Catholic community has suffered grievously – past tense. But my belief that discrimination against Catholics had become a thing of the past has, I am sorry to say, had to be revised. Conversations and examination of readily-available statistics relating to employment and opportunity in the North, tell a disturbing story of continuing discrimination which is the more insidious for being masked by protestations to the contrary on the part of those in high places. I hoped and expected to find otherwise.

Similarly, my desire, surely held by most English people, to hear and to think well of our armed services, has taken some severe knocks. It is certainly true that the army, for more than twenty-five years, has done a superb professional job, and great personal courage has been required in doing it. Yet I have been given verbal and written evidence of serious misconduct by British soldiers, particularly in predominantly Catholic areas. This is sufficient to suggest, even to moderate and otherwise well-disposed citizens, that some soldiers, at least, have come to regard all Roman Catholics as 'the enemy'. Suspicion of collusion with (or at best a blind eye turned towards) Protestant paramilitaries only fuels the flames of resentment. Perceived instances of favourable treatment given to service personnel convicted of grave crimes only makes matters worse. These conclusions distress me, but I have the highest regard for the integrity of my informants on these matters.

The pain of the Catholic community, especially those of nationalist or republican sympathies, has often been stated, and is very real. For my own part, I concur with the view of Monsignor Denis Faul, a courageous and often outspoken priest, who has said of the British: 'Until they repent of what they have done and make amends for what they have done, there will never be peace here.'[6]

NOTHING BUT OLD ENGLAND

Another of my prejudgements has, however, been exposed as superficial and unfair. I have never found it easy to understand or justify the actions and attitudes of the Northern Protestants. Consequently I have belittled and spoken ill of them. I regret that very much. My attitude was not helped when I was duped into persuading my colleagues at Liverpool Cathedral to invite a seemingly innocent organization to hold a special service there. On the day, they turned out to be more than a thousand Orangemen, whose orange sashes were produced during the opening hymn! Yet my conversations have caused me to re-evaluate many of my attitudes, even though the capacity of the unionist community to shoot itself in the foot and alienate public sympathy is quite extraordinary.

It has saddened me that so few Protestants in the North seem able to talk coherently about the positive virtues of their community, and even fewer are willing to examine their history, beyond sloganizing about siege, surrender and Rome Rule. This gives even the most highly articulate among them an appearance of bombast and arrogance which is completely at odds with the vulnerability and insecurity beneath the surface. There is, I believe, another story to tell, and a better one.

The Protestants seem to have less sense of history than the Catholics. Although they are full of the memory of particular defining events, especially 1689 and 1691, and the heroic and embattled qualities which were displayed, their view of the sweep of their history is very restricted. Perhaps this is because they have come to realize that their story must seem unappealing to the outsider: as Sir Robert Southwell wrote in 1699, 'those . . . Protestants who have nothing on this side of Paradise to adhere to but old England.'[7]

It is true that 'old England' has planted them, used them and abused them, and above all made them dependant. This is the principal reason why they have never needed, nor wanted, to investigate their roots in the manner that has been so crucial to their more obviously dispossessed Catholic neighbours. It is true that when the Protestants had power – albeit a very conditional kind of power – they abused it shamefully. Yet it is possible to feel real sympathy for the experiences of their community, not least in the civil war of the 1920s, and the remorseless campaign of republican terrorism in the 1970s and 80s, which struck fear into the Protestant people, and has resulted in continuing and increasing recruitment to their own paramilitaries. It is possible to read words of Kevin O'Higgins from 1925 as if they were spoken seventy years later: 'And now we wonder why the Orangemen are not hopping like so many fleas across the border in their anxiety to come within our fold and jurisdiction.'[8]

It is indeed a tragedy that, in the quest for a genuinely Irish identity at the time of O'Connell, this came to be associated so exclusively with Catholicism. Later, when special arrangements were being considered for the Northern Protestants, Parnell was well aware of the dangers, declaring: 'We want the energy, the patriotism, the talents and work of every Irishman.'[9] To which, after my own encounters, I would wish to add the witness to biblical values and personal moral responsibility which, at its best, the Protestant community of Ulster is capable of demonstrating.

The one distinctive feature of the settlers was their Protestant faith: indeed, this was the pre-condition of their being given land, so it was inevitable that this should become politicized. Consequently, when a scapegoat was sought for their own ills, it was not upon nationalism or republicanism as such that they lighted, but upon Catholicism; and it must be said that the Roman Catholic Church has not always been reluctant to provide them with suitable material.

Leaving aside the extraordinary period of Presbyterian-Catholic co-operation, when both faced persecution in the late eighteenth century, this has made inevitable the 'Home Rule – Rome Rule' slogans in the twentieth, which still provide a real, if now largely anachronistic, rallying-cry for the Protestant community. There has never been the need for Protestants to look deeply into their history, to examine their roots. Now, however, they face a new and alarming situation – not new, perhaps, in their own perception, but new in the sense that it has been made explicit by a British government. This novelty is the declaration that Britain no longer has any interest whatsoever in staying in Northern Ireland if the people living there no longer wish it. To the Protestant community, that is tantamount to saying 'We have outlived our usefulness'.

In the light of this shocking revelation (which almost certainly accords with the view of most of the British people, though for instinctive rather than considered reasons) it may be that the Protestant community, if it is not to be left entirely high and dry, will need to look more closely at its roots, in order to discover where its future interests might best be served.

Terence Brown, in a very interesting essay, *The Whole Protestant Community*, argues this compellingly:

> A people who have known resistance as well as dissent, rebellion, dispute, religious enthusiasm in the midst of rural and urban deprivation, have an interesting story to tell themselves – one of essential homelessness, dependency, anxiety, obdurate fantasising, sacrifices in the name of history, villainous political opportunism, moments of idealistic aspiration.[10]

The connections, in the discovery of their roots, with the Irish

Catholic community are extraordinarily important. Brown goes further, and in doing so, must alarm many who are as yet unready to press the matter this far. He suggests that, in telling this story, the Protestant people may begin to realize where they are most at home, where they really belong, and with whom they share that home.

A COMMON BOND

One of my correspondents, a Roman Catholic priest who feels particularly impelled to pray for reconciliation and seek God's will for Ireland, suggested:

> The Irish people North and South are a Celtic people, and underneath their differences is a common bond. This common bond is buried in their unconscious personal and collective lives. The land has a powerful effect on the psyche and lives of its people. I believe that the two peoples are destined to share the land and society together.

Alarming as such thinking may be, the peace process has made it both possible and necessary to examine all possibilities, even those which have hitherto been declared 'off limits', for circumstances alter cases. As an unnamed source in the Northern Ireland Office said at the time of the Declaration, 'Everything is now up for grabs'.

It is to be hoped that at least there may emerge the will and the courage to examine all possible options, which the changed situation necessitates and perhaps facilitates. This, of course, brings us once again to the overwhelming aspect of fear which dogs both communities in Northern Ireland, and which has coloured so much of what I have been told. Jackie Redpath has written that the 'siege mentality' which has always been at the heart of Ulster Protestantism has, in the past twenty-five years, become 'a psychological, cultural, intellectual, political, physical and economic retreat.'[11]

Criticism of either community in Northern Ireland from outside is resented. That makes recent comments by Timothy Kinahan especially significant, for he is a Church of Ireland

Rector, working in east Belfast. Having posed the question, what does it mean to be a Protestant Christian in Northern Ireland today, he continues:

> Is it a Christian merit to cling to supposed privilege? Is it a Christian merit to refuse to talk with those enemies that Christ told us to love? Was it a Christian merit to dismiss for seventy-five years the nationalist cries of alienation and pleas for justice?
>
> Is it now a Christian merit to expect others to hear our cries of 'foul' when we ignored theirs for so long? Is it a Christian merit to seek for a return to a Stormont-type 'majority rule' . . . while angrily denouncing any suggestion of a united Ireland (which is, after all, only majority rule in a different and geographically more logical context)?[12]

Those are very brave words. Many will find it impossible to hear or heed their message because they are afraid. This all-pervasive fear was well expressed to me in a letter from a descendant of the old Church of Ireland ascendancy who is committed to seeking new ways of reconciliation. He wrote:

> We here are in the iron-like grip of control: control of history, of present fears, prejudices and hatred; the control which resists the pain of truth and the change involved; the control which refuses to take Christ seriously . . . Here we have a situation which is glaringly out of control, unmanageable, where no-one knows the way out.

That last statement has the ring of authenticity about it. It echoes words of Bishop John Baker:

> There is no rational step forward which is not open to fatal objections, not least because of the element of moral justification for the hard line taken by each side . . . Theologically it bears the distinguishing mark of evil, namely that there is no right answer to the problem it poses.[13]

LOOKING BEYOND FEAR

The unexpected can only happen when risks are taken, and especially the risk of letting go of control. Only then can unexpected relationships of trust be forged; only then can it become permissible to discuss the unthinkable with those one has hitherto regarded as unspeakable, as Nelson Mandela and F. W. de Klerk, Rabin and Arafat, and Sadat and Begin at an earlier time, among others, have demonstrated. Mandela, indeed, on the specific issue of Northern Ireland, in words which many will have found embarrassing, but which may be felt to have been vindicated by the South African experience, said in 1990: 'What we should like to see is that the British government and the IRA should adopt precisely the line we have taken with regard to our own internal situation. There is nothing better than opponents sitting down to resolve problems in a peaceful manner.'[14]

Perhaps the contribution which British, and especially English people can make is to sit down with those who regard themselves as British, and begin to build a new relationship. This will involve seeking and affirming their real strengths, looking more deeply than the fear and the bombast to what one Presbyterian minister described to me as 'the gold within'. That can only be done in penitence and humility. Indeed, it might be attempted, not on the basis of any sort of superiority, but rather on the basis of our own needs, at a time when so many of the institutions in British society are under threat. The strong convictions and basic moral values of the Protestant people of Northern Ireland represent aspects of life which we are in danger of losing. We need them, just as I was frequently told the Irish Republic needs them as well.

For me, then, it will be apparent that the Protestants present an agonizing dilemma. The English-Catholic nationalist relationship I can understand, in all its pain and injustice. It is essentially straightforward; the injury is as plain as it is horrible. The Protestants, in all the complexity of their defensiveness and enforced dependency, are something else altogether. Yet I have a deep sense that our relationship with them is the key to future progress.

If I have seemed to labour the need for understanding of the predicament of the Northern Protestant community, it is not without cause. I am sure that the Protestants, by virtue of their historical associations with Britain, which are certainly too intimate to be unravelled carelessly, if at all, are no less deserving of

understanding than their Catholic cousins. Both have been dam-
aged. Both are victims.

BODY AND SOUL

Joan Tapsfield is an English woman, now over eighty years of age,
who chose to move to Northern Ireland eighteen years ago to
examine her own country's history in Ireland. She wrote about
her experiences in *An English Pilgrim in Northern Ireland*.[15] In her
own way, Joan has tried to make amends for some of the hurt
which has been done to the people of Ireland. She does not regard
this as in any way disloyal or unpatriotic. Indeed, she says, true
patriotism must be rooted in truth, which is not necessarily truth
as the Establishment wishes it to be received. 'To face the past is
not to forego our patriotism, but to enhance it.'
Joan speaks of deep things with deceptive ease and simplicity.
When I called to have tea with her, she said this:

> The damage we have done to the Roman Catholics is to the
> body, and to the Protestants, to the soul. The Catholics were
> made to suffer terrible physical hardships – evictions, neglect,
> famine, dreadful things; so many died.
>
> The Protestants' ills were social. Having given them power,
> having been rewarded by their support and sacrifice in two
> world wars, especially the first, we told them we had no further
> interest in them – in effect, we don't care any more. To say to
> a friend 'we no longer want you' is terribly damaging to the
> spirit.
>
> That is why there can be no possibility of justice to both
> communities without penitence, because true and real peni-
> tence leaves no room for blame. Yes, of course the Stormont
> unionists did wrong – very wrong; yes, of course the IRA have
> done terrible things, but as long as we just *blame*, we cannot
> understand.
>
> The Church of England has a vital role. It is very difficult for
> the Irish churches to admit they have been – or done – wrong,
> for understandable historical reasons, but the Church of
> England is the guardian of the soul of the nation. It has a duty

to inform and to lead. What British, and especially English people cannot do is to demand that people in Ireland change, because of the way Britain has behaved – our superiority is the worst sin of all.[16]

Joan Tapsfield, and many others from every tradition in both parts of Ireland, attach great importance to the role of the churches, both in everyday life and as an indispensable part of any solution to the troubles. I am conscious that much of what I have reported has been implicitly critical of the churches in Ireland. I have no right to make those criticisms my own, and I refrain from doing so. Yet if it is true that the religious divisions in Ireland, and especially in the North, are at the heart of society's divisions, then it cannot be wrong to suggest that the churches have to be in the vanguard of change, the essential precursor of which is openness to one another.

The structures for ecumenical co-operation bridge the Irish Sea: the main agency for unity is the Council of Churches for Britain and Ireland; but there is a lack of perceived urgency about the matter in Britain. Although progress in Ireland has been patchy, more attempts have been made there to initiate dialogue than in Britain. It is critical for the English churches to wake up to this need, and perhaps, because of their leading role in ecumenism, the churches in Liverpool must give a lead, or a more energetic one.

Religion is about the antithesis of fear. Indeed, the defining text of this book, which has recurred frequently, is that there is no room for fear in love; perfect love casts out fear. That fear, in Northern Ireland, is principally fear of the unknown. I have been shocked to hear deeply-prejudiced remarks, both in the North and the Republic, from people who occupy positions of such trust and responsibility within the churches that I cannot withhold the judgement that they ought to know better. But the same is true in Britain, though here it usually takes the form of patronizing attitudes on the part of those of us who hold office in the Established Church.

It is amusing but instructive to record a conversation I had over dinner with a Frenchman, who works in some obscure department of the European Community in Strasbourg. He told me he finds the English impossible to understand. I asked him: 'Is it the effortless superiority we seem to display towards foreigners?' He replied: 'Non, non.. If it was without effort, it would not matter, but you work at it so very hard.'

SECURITY AND IDENTITY

The Kingdom of God is about conflict. Scripture contains many references to it – indeed, it underlies so much of the Old and New Testaments. Conflict is about victors and victims, acceptance and rejection. In the Old Testament, particularly the accounts of Israel and her neighbours, we see that the good person, the good nation, is apt to be shunned, and that that is very unpleasant. In the gospels of the New Testament, Jesus himself, in spite of (or, with hindsight, because of) his actions and his words, was shunned to the point of a horrific fate. But he did not revile; he somehow absorbed all the pain, all the hostility, all the viciousness.

It is easy to say it was different for him, because he was somehow above it all, divine – easy but ill-judged. Jesus behaved as he did because his sense of his own identity was secure. He came to realize, through the unimaginable agony of self-doubt and longing, that he was to do his Father's will. Thus, and only thus, was he able to meet duplicity with quiet dignity, earthly authority with divine wisdom, and an unspeakable death with words of forgiveness.

Personal security comes with identity. It eluded the earliest disciples who, within hours of 'Father, forgive' were locked in an upper room, just another scared human group. They came to understand, though we their successors often forget, that the Church exists to represent God, and that it best does that when its members, and especially its leaders, are secure enough in their own identity to let go of feelings of anger, anxiety, violence and bitterness, and point to a God who is in the midst, in all his majesty and vulnerability. Indeed, the ecumenical process, as Alan Falconer has pointed out, 'involves embracing that vulnerability with regard to each other which is evident in the life, ministry, death and resurrection of Jesus Christ.'[17]

Much of what I have written has been an attempt to justify the contention that politics alone cannot bring lasting peace to Ireland. Indeed, I would go further and say that human means alone are insufficient. I am keenly aware of the derision which such a claim invites, particularly at a time when the Church, and the spiritual values which it exists to uphold and promote, are under sustained attack from many quarters.

Sorrow and penitence are basic to a Christian understanding of life. They are also essential prerequisites of healthy personal relationships. Sorrow and penitence, whether expressed by one human being towards another in recognition of hurtful words or actions, or by the official representative of one nation or people towards another for similar reasons, are utterly unconditional. They invite reciprocal forgiveness: they cannot justly demand it.

I have tried to demonstrate that there are useful contemporary examples of such unconditional expressions of regret, and desire to make amends. It will not be easy to apply the same criteria to the issue of Britain and Ireland. Lord Hylton, an independent peer with a lifelong interest in Northern Ireland, wrote to the Prime Minister, Margaret Thatcher, in 1981, urging just such a full-hearted apology for past actions:

> As Rabbi D. J. Goldberg put it in *The Times* of May 6th 1981, only the victims can release the aggressors from guilt, and he said 'the greater thing is never to forget, yet also to forgive' . . . I believe that the time has come for Britain to face up to and ask forgiveness for the immense wrongs it has done to the people of Ireland . . . A public declaration that Britain has much to answer for in respect of Ireland over the past four centuries and indeed needs forgiveness for past injustices would, I believe, be of great value now.[18]

Lord Hylton's appeal, which fell on deaf ears, stressed that such a gesture would not disarm the terrorists or bring about instant solutions. It would, however, influence 'the fair-minded and peace-loving majority in both countries, and in both main communities in Ulster. It would also help to isolate the terrorists.'

This last point seems to me to be critical. I have heard and read much in Britain about 'mindless' violence, but not in Ireland. There I have found sober, even chilling realism about the terrorists. I have heard doctors and psychiatrists say that terrorists in Northern Ireland are not mentally sick, nor psychopathic personalities. They are normal, family-loving people, many of them church-goers, who in normal circumstances would not harm anyone or anything. Their circumstances are not normal. They believe themselves either to be at war or to be legitimately defending all that they hold dear. As such, they are able with a clear conscience to suspend all the normal restraints, and behave in a way which defies the imagination of those who are not involved, or who have not heard them speak. For the terrorists, indeed, the end does justify the means.

Nothing could be more important than that people in Britain understand this; not (God forbid) that we should seek to condone what has been done, but to understand the futility of digging ever deeper with every outrage into the vocabulary of condemnation and incomprehension. Desperately hard though it is – and perhaps impossible for some of those who have been personally scarred in body or mind by unspeakable acts – we have to understand the weight of anger and bitterness which still fills the hearts of many in Northern Ireland, and which the peace process has only conditionally suppressed.

WRONGED AND WRONGDOERS

'Enough is Enough' is more than the slogan of a peace movement: it reflects the deeply-felt conviction of the overwhelming majority of the people most involved. Yet, as history and theology show, it is impossible to make peace with oppression, to ignore injustice, or to seek cheap forgiveness and expect the result to be a sustainable peace. I continue to believe that a full, generous and imaginative apology by Britain to both communities in Ireland for its actions over 800 years would be a profoundly Christian act, understood by people of all faiths, and would open up the possibility of a new beginning. It would also be widely admired throughout the world, and not least in those countries to which Ireland is especially linked through emigration.

Archbishop Desmond Tutu, whose role in the bringing to birth of the new South Africa has been considerable, and an inspiration beyond the confines of the Anglican Communion, has written that the need for repentance and forgiveness is, 'indispensable for getting right relationships between those who have been wronged and the wrongdoers within nations and between nations. Unless you deal with the past in a creative and positive manner, then you run the terrible risk of having no future worth speaking about.'[19]

Brian Frost has been involved in the ecumenical movement for more than thirty years, and ran the Forgiveness and Politics Study Project of the British Council of Churches. Addressing an ecumenical meeting in the Wirral early in 1994, he concluded his address with these words: 'There is really only one question in all this: have we the will, the political, spiritual, theological and managerial will, to make something happen, and the wisdom and acumen to release us all from the burden of our histories?'[20] In his book *The Politics of Peace*, Frost gives the lie to those who would claim that such sentiments belong only to the rarefied atmosphere of the churches: 'Perhaps God's activity is to be found hidden in the life of the world as well as within the churches, that part of Society which has recognised and responded to the significance and purpose of Jesus.'[21]

The Christian attributes of sorrow, penitence and penance are themselves paralleled by very secular ones: guilt, contrition and remedial action. There must be a way to apply these, in a national context, to the relationship between Britain and Ireland. The situation presents something of a paradox, in that we have what is in essence a British problem – pain inflicted for selfish ends – yet a political solution to the ensuing divisions can only rest, ultimately, with the people who live in the island of Ireland.

Yet it must be for Britain to make the first move. If the many people who have written or talked to me are sane, sensible and constructive in what they have said or written, then I must have not only hope, but optimism. We in Britain who do not move in what a correspondent called 'the circles of power and influence' can nevertheless do much to help. We can read and learn, and badger those who do move in such circles. We can encourage active co-operation between our own professional associations, churches, trade unions, colleges, clubs – institutions of all kinds – with others in Ireland, the North and the Republic. We can visit

both parts of Ireland. I defy anyone to witness the security measures in Belfast and Derry, at least until early in 1995 ('more intru-
sive than anything I have seen in the third world, South Africa
included,' as Chris Brazier has written)[22] and not be shaken
rigid by the realization that this land, politically speaking, is our
land.

The churches in Northern Ireland and the Republic (most of
which operate in an all-Ireland context) need the help of English
Christians. They need to be affirmed, supported and helped to see
that if they could apply themselves single-mindedly to the pursuit
of peace, if they could rid themselves of those expressions of
prejudice which belong to an earlier era, then the most immense
energy would be released. Ireland needs healing, not victory, and
healing should be the preoccupation of all who call themselves
Christian. The churches in Ireland must break out of their prisons
and discover, perhaps for the first time, the voice of prophecy.

British (and especially English) Christians can show the way, if
we have the will, by remedying our ignorance of history, and by
accepting, painful as it is, that all have sinned and fallen short of
the grace of God, beginning with ourselves. The Church of
England, for better or worse, is the Established Church of the
nation. For all the considerations of etiquette and propriety
towards other churches, for all the desire not to seem to be inter-
fering, the Church of England has a unique responsibility and
opportunity to give a lead.

THE DOOR OF JUSTICE

Canon Naim Ateek is a Palestinian and an Anglican priest. His
profound book *Justice and only Justice* has grown out of decades of
conflict and the complexity of daily living within the land which
all three great world faiths regard as holy. He concludes that the
only way to peace in his homeland lies in an insistence upon
justice, and the responsibility of loving our neighbour as ourself.
The role of the Christian church should be prophecy and peace-
making. He points to countries at loggerheads with each other –
doors slammed in each other's faces – and concludes:

Peace is knocking at our door, but the door has not been opened. The door of peace is reached only through the door of justice. Once that door opens, peace lies inside. Where peace is, a meal is prepared; it is the feast of reconciliation ready to be celebrated. There is, however, no entrance except through the door of justice. This hope is not imaginary, it is real. It is accessible. It is within reach. It demands courage . . .

To keep struggling against hate and to practise forgiveness need not mean abdicating one's rights or renouncing justice. This should be emphasised over and over again. It is part of loving one's enemy that Christians must remind the 'enemy' of justice and right. It is part of loving to speak the truth. It is part of our responsibility to ourselves and to God's people in the world to expose injustice. What is wrong is wrong. What is unjust is unjust.[23]

13 *There is another way*

In the middle of a pile of much-thumbed magazines in my doctor's waiting room, I came across a torn fragment of paper. I could not identify the magazine from which it had come, but I concluded, with the capacity to rationalize coincidence that is the hallmark of people of faith, that I was intended to find it.

> The dirty Irish war could have been solved by men of vision years ago, but it needs the kind of gigantic leap of imagination that a genius makes in science, a quantum leap of thinking that leaves conventional thought behind.

Profound, if for me anonymous, words; yet even men of vision cannot solve conflicts on their own. Their vision has to strike a matching chord in the people they lead or represent. 'The people' were defined by Richard Wagner in his introduction to *Die Meistersinger* as 'the epitome of all those who share a common need'. The common need of all who live in Ireland, and of all who live in the United Kingdom, is peace.

Nothing could be more urgent than that the common need for peace should be recognized in Britain, and our apathy towards unpleasant realities across the water overcome. We are all involved. It is an axiom of medicine that healing lies in understanding the sickness, identifying the pain and sticking with it, and never ceasing to ask the hard questions. That is the responsibility of people of good will in Britain, and Christian people in particular.

In these past months, I have made an attempt to understand the conflict within Ireland, and between Britain and the peoples there. In some respects, I am now more confused than when I began, but in others, two in particular, I can now see with greater clarity.

First, each community in Northern Ireland is imprisoned by its memories, and because those memories are held in isolation, they cannot be healed, and the communities are unable to face the future together. It is very hard for someone from outside to grasp this. Yet it is clear that the historical events, and the cultural memories which they inspire, have got to be addressed if they are not to be endlessly re-processed and used to build (literally) higher and higher walls against 'the other'. Maya Angelou was surely right:

> History, despite its wrenching pain,
> Cannot be unlived, but if faced
> With courage, need not be lived again.[1]

The second point of clarity for me concerns the churches. Many people, and who can blame them, are very intolerant of the part which religion has played in the conflict, and thoroughly dismissive of any suggestion that the churches might contribute to the cause of peace. I can well understand such frustration: after all, our Christian denominations, with their worldly standards, their preoccupation with success as the world judges it, seem a very long way from the Man of Nazareth who died an ignominious death, breathing words of forgiveness.

Yet it is that very vulnerability at the heart of the Christian faith, symbolized by the cross, which provides a glimmer of hope. Whenever Christians meet for worship, they listen to the Word of God, the stories of God's liberating power in the Old and New Testaments. And whenever they commemorate the Lord's Supper, liturgically or with great simplicity, they remember Jesus Christ, the victim. More than that, in a special and intimate way they make those events present in the here and now, and in so doing make possible a new beginning.

Of all people, members of the Christian churches ought to know how to remember.[2] In doing so, they – we – may begin to understand the necessity and the power of repentance and the unconditional nature of forgiveness. We may also come to understand the need to be vulnerable if we are to do Christ's will. In our weakness lies our strength. That is why the churches are central to the solution of the conflict in Northern Ireland: *they know how to remember,* and this gives them the primary resource to reconcile the fractured memories of a community in conflict.

Freedom from fear is the heart of the Christian gospel, and the very least that English Christians should do is to pray in as active and informed a way as possible that their sisters and brothers in Ireland might be delivered from their very real fears. The churches must be helped, in all their historical richness and diversity, to proclaim and to live the gospel. The very conflict which exists between them, at least in the perception of many of their members, may itself become fruitful for change. Martin Marty has written:

> Conflict is to be overcome, not by suppressing differences, stomping on freedom, dishonouring will or refusing to listen to voice. Conflict is used to stimulate the imagination, quicken pulses for adventure and force the persons and parties to take on ideas and tasks so great that they become newly reliant on God . . . 'that you be united in the same mind and purpose', or at least, as with all things on the earthly side of the heavenly kingdom, always be 'in the process of being united' because Christ was and is not divided.[3]

POSTSCRIPT

My last word must be a very personal one. I cannot travel the open spaces of Ireland, particularly in the west, without experiencing, amidst the rugged beauty, a deep sense of the oppression of the past. I think of the countless people who lie buried there, for the most part unclaimed, unremembered, unprayed over, their stories untold. The concept of the spirit-world is today often derided as medieval superstition, yet a pall of suffering which is almost tangible seems to hang over the land, and to cry out for release.

I have been much moved by *The Hidden Ireland*, written by Daniel Corkery in 1924.[4] It is a study of the eighteenth-century Gaelic poets, 'from an Irish, human, not literary angle, to try to reach the soul of the people'.

Corkery quotes from a poem which is attributed to Eoghan Ó Súilleabháin:

> Tis not the poverty I most detest,
> Nor being down for ever,
> But the insult that follows it
> Which no leeches can cure.

The book ends with words of Alice Stopford Green:

> To them [the Irish] has been meted out the second death – the lot feared beyond all else by men of honour. They have been buried by the false hands of strangers in the deep pit of contempt, reproach and forgetfulness – an unmerited grave of silence and shame.

Politics and peace processes, even when conducted with integrity and the best of intentions, can take us so far, and no further. True and lasting reconciliation, which is of God, and passes all understanding, depends upon something deeper and even more demanding. It requires that we tread the costly road of sorrow and penitence; and it requires, perhaps above all else, constant and informed prayer. I dare to believe that this way will, in the end, prevail, for it is God's way. Susan Ruach reminds us that it is also, for many of us, a new way:

> To struggle used to be
> To grab with both hands
> and shake
> and twist
> and turn
> and push
> and shove and not give in
> But wrest an answer from it all
> As Jacob did a blessing.
>
> But there is another way
> To struggle with an issue, a question –
> Simply to jump
> off
> into the abyss
> and find ourselves
> floating

falling
tumbling
being led
slowly and gently
but surely
to the answers God has for us –
to watch the answers unfold
before our eyes and still
to be a part of the unfolding.

But, oh! the trust
necessary for this new way!
Not to be always reaching out
For the old hand-holds.[5]

Appendix One
An outline of Irish history

IN THE BEGINNING

The first inhabitants of Ireland arrived about eight thousand years ago in the middle Stone Age, probably from Scotland. Little is known about these earliest settlers. It is the people of the neolithic period – the 'modern' Stone Age – who have left more evidence of their way of life. They were able to cultivate the land and raise cattle. They left behind them enormous passage graves, dolmen tombs and standing-stone circles, all of these pre-dating the pyramids of Egypt.

THE CELTS

The Celts arrived around the fifth century BC. They came from central Europe, bringing with them to Ireland the skill of iron-making, and thus superiority in weapons. They also brought a love of learning, and great artistic ability and imagination, particularly in jewellery and textiles.

In mainland Europe, the Romans drove the Celts to the edges of the continent, but never got as far as Ireland, hence the survival there of Celtic language and culture.

THE COMING OF CHRISTIANITY

Around the beginning of the Christian era, Ireland seems to have consisted of more than one hundred small gathered communities, grouped into five major kingdoms. In time, these were formed into two groups, Tara in the north and Munster in the south, each with a high king. Eventually, around AD 400, the King of Tara came to be recognized as king of the whole of Ireland, though probably with little real authority.

As early as the middle of the fifth century, Ireland was being converted to Christianity. The 'Apostle of the Irish' was Patrick, a Roman citizen who came to Ireland as a slave, and escaped to Europe. He felt called by God to convert the Irish people to Christianity. Patrick was made a bishop in Gaul, and returned to Ireland in 432.

Over an extraordinarily short period, perhaps thirty years, he succeeded in evangelizing the whole island, with co-operation from local kings. By the middle of the sixth century, Ireland was a fully-fledged province of the Western Church. It is probable that a number of stories and traditions have been combined by later hands – there may, indeed, have been more than one 'Patrick'.

The fact remains, however, that at this early date, the Irish Church possessed skilful and imaginative leadership, whether or not this and later developments were attributed to Patrick in order to give them legitimacy. Attempts were made to organize the Irish Church in the same way as others in the Roman empire; these had dioceses which were centred on cathedrals in large towns, each presided over by a bishop. However, there were no such urban centres in Ireland, so a different system evolved. This was monasticism.

THE MONASTERIES

Monasteries appeared all over the country, usually taking the form of wooden huts clustered around a stone church, of which the remains of a number still exist. The only complete stone church still in existence is Gallarus' Oratory in Kerry, the oldest building of its type in Europe, dating from the seventh century. The monasteries were centres of learning, a characteristic no doubt inherited from the Celts. The monks, who lived simple and austere lives, sought to bring the light of Christ into the prevailing darkness.

Art and literature flourished in the monastic age. The Book of Kells is a particularly fine example of monastic craftsmanship – an illuminated manuscript of the New Testament, dating from the eighth century. A number of characteristic high crosses have also survived, bearing sculptured scenes from the Bible as aids to instruction, and tall round towers. The Irish monasteries became sought-after centres of learning, and drew thousands of students from Britain and Europe, hence the well-known definition of Ireland, which dates from the monastic period, *'Insula sanctorum et doctorum'* – an island of holy and learned men.

THE VIKINGS

The first Viking raid on Ireland came in the mid-790s. The raiders, who came from Scandinavia, first plundered eastern coastal communities, and then went on to destroy many of the monasteries, stealing objects of value and destroying libraries. At the same time, however, the Vikings inaugurated a period of construction, founding towns such as Dublin in 841, and then Limerick, Waterford, Wexford and Cork.

The Vikings were not seriously challenged, since the scattered kingdoms had no centralized military organization. Early in the eleventh century, however, Brian Boru became High King, and mobilized an effective army. In 1014 the native Irish army did battle with the Vikings at Clontarf, and were victorious. The military supremacy of the invaders was broken. Many, however, remained and adapted to the local way of life.

THE NORMANS

England was ruled by the Normans in the twelfth century, and in 1169 an army of knights sent by King Henry II invaded Ireland, and captured Waterford, Wexford and Dublin. Henry himself came, with the blessing of the Pope, Adrian IV, who was Anglo-Norman. Once the English crown obtained a foothold in Ireland, the Anglo-Normans sought to control all the people, and there began a series of conflicts involving the English crown and the various peoples of Ireland, which have characterized each of the past eight centuries.

The Anglo-Normans built castles, cathedrals, large fortified houses and monasteries. They never succeeded in controlling the whole country, partly because they brought insufficient troops, but also because they adapted rapidly to Irish ways, intermarrying and adopting the local language.

This became a real anxiety to the English crown, which tried to prevent further assimilation by passing the Statutes of Kilkenny in 1366. The Irish language was prohibited for the colonists, who were no longer permitted to intermarry or play the same games as the natives. The process of integration had gone too far, however, and in many cases local alliances were formed between the native population and their former adversaries. The Irish and the Anglo-Normans now both opposed Crown influence in Ireland.

In 1429, Henry VI, in order to try to impose order on the country, gave generous grants for the building of castles, the dimensions of which were laid down, and these appeared all over the land – more than a thousand of them. Their ruins may be seen to this day.

By 1500 the Crown controlled only a small strip of land around Dublin, known as 'the Pale'. Regulations forbade local chiefs to hold forces without the permission of the crown's representative. This, and the enforced surrender of lands, which could be received back only under stringent terms and conditions, sowed seeds of deep bitterness.

HENRY VIII

Political turmoil ensued throughout the fifteenth century. Henry VIII succeeded to the throne in 1509. He determined to rule Ireland through his representative in Dublin, instead of through local overlords, whose loyalty could not be relied upon. He forced local kings to adopt anglicized titles in place of their native ones.

Measures such as these were deeply resented, but far more resentment was caused by the enforced introduction, following the Reformation in England, of the 'new Protestant faith'. The Reformation never penetrated to Ireland except via the English crown, and the Irish and their Norman conquerors were united in adherence to the old Catholic faith, though in point of fact many pagan and superstitious practices continued, particularly in the more remote areas.

THE PLANTATIONS

Queen Mary's short reign (1553–58) was characterized by the enforced colonization of Offaly and Leix (King's and Queen's counties), with 'planted' settlers. This policy of enforced settlement continued with new vigour under Elizabeth I, who was determined to protect England from Spain.

The Irish sought assistance from Philip II of Spain, but the Spanish Armada was defeated in 1588 off the west coast of Ireland by a combination of the English fleet and the weather. The Irish, under Hugh O'Neill, in spite of the support of 4,000 Spanish troops, were defeated by the English army at Kinsale in 1601.

O'Neill, having signed a treaty which committed the Irish to obey English law and follow English customs, fled with other earls and their followers to exile in Europe. This 'flight of the earls' resulted in Ireland losing its indigenous Gaelic leaders, and made possible a strong English administration from Dublin.

Over 300,000 acres of land had been given to English settlers in Munster. The plantation of Ulster began in 1609, with the bulk of settlers arriving after 1650. (There is evidence of some much earlier Scots settlement in medieval centuries). The new settlers were introduced from England and Scotland, now united under one king. All were Protestant - the Scots, Presbyterian. All were required to take an oath of allegiance to Protestantism before they were given land.

Most of the native Irish were driven from the best land in the north, though some remained to work for the new settlers. Much of Ireland was by this time in a condition of near-destitution – contemporary accounts speak of widespread poverty and starvation. The deep resentment caused by the seizure of land, compounded by the religious divide, engendered bitter conflict which has endured to this day, particularly in the north.

CROMWELL IN IRELAND

This bitterness against the usurpers spilled over into rebellion in 1641. Perhaps as many as 12,000 settlers died, mainly from hunger and exposure. These deaths, and the retribution that followed,

mark 1641 out as a key date in the developing insecurity of the
settlers, and the bitter resentment of each other by both sides. The
rebellion was put down, but full retribution awaited the arrival of
Oliver Cromwell after the Civil War in England.

Cromwell came to visit 'the righteous judgement of God' upon
the Irish in 1649. His army massacred virtually the entire population of Drogheda, which had refused to surrender to him, and a
similar event occurred at Wexford, after which most towns surrendered. More land was taken from Catholics, and given as payment to English officers and Cromwell's staff. The ruthlessness of
Cromwell's short time in Ireland is still burned deep in the Irish
memory.

Even greater confiscation of land followed, the Catholic owners
being driven west 'to hell or Connacht'. Cromwell professed the
Christian faith, and his letters and writings indicate that he saw his
campaign of slaughter as a divine mission. By the time Cromwell
left, more than 600,000 Irish had died, as a result of conflict, dis-
ease or starvation. Most of those who survived lost their lands, and
100,000 were deported as slaves, mainly to the West Indies. In
Ulster, no land at all remained in Catholic hands by 1680 (though
about one in nine of the Protestant population at this time were
of Irish Catholic origin, having converted to the Protestant faith).
The population of Ireland had virtually halved.

A CATHOLIC MONARCH

The accession of the Catholic James II to the English throne in
1685 seemed to provide some hope of change, as he set out to
restore the Catholic faith throughout his kingdoms. Many Irish
people supported him in his attempt to keep his throne against
William of Orange, his Dutch son-in-law, who had been invited
by the aristocracy and merchants in England to become king.

James and William met in battle in County Meath at the Battle
of the Boyne, on 12 July 1690. The Protestants won the day, due
to a combination of James's poor military leadership and personal
cowardice, and to the numerical superiority of the Protestant
forces. The Boyne was followed by an even bloodier encounter at
Aughrim the following year. To this day the commemoration of

the Battle of the Boyne is the most important anniversary for the Protestants in Ulster, and is associated with the memory of brave resistance in the sieges of Derry and Enniskillen.

These victories effectively broke the remaining power of the old Gaelic culture, which, in effect, went underground, and also of the few remaining Catholic landowners. It is true that some Catholic rights were restored in the Treaty of Limerick later in 1691, but only on the condition that the garrison at Limerick, together with the chief leaders of the Irish army, went abroad to France.

THE PENAL LAWS

The lull was short-lived. From 1691 onwards, 'Penal Laws' were enacted by the Irish parliament, which was composed exclusively of members of the Church of Ireland. These laws prohibited Catholics from holding any office of state, standing for parliament, entering the legal profession or holding commissions in the armed forces. Of greater long-term significance, Catholics were also forbidden to buy land or to bequeath it without restriction. The result was that by 1775 a bare five per cent of the island of Ireland remained in Catholic ownership.

The Penal Laws affected dissenting (i.e. non-Anglican) Protestants as well. Presbyterians were subject to prohibitions, and were not permitted to celebrate marriages. Overall, however, and for a longer period, the Catholics were the worst affected. The intention, indeed, was to eradicate the Catholic faith in Ireland (though with the parallel intention of securing earlier land confiscations) but religious prohibitions were impossible to enforce in a country which was overwhelmingly of the Roman Catholic obedience. The secular exclusions, though, prevented Catholics from attaining significant advancement in any sphere of public life.

A great gulf now existed between the rulers and the ruled. Protestant landowners (the 'ascendancy') built fine houses, isolated from their employees. From these they exacted rent, often in the form of produce, which they then exported to England. Few landlords were noted for public service or social awareness.

The poor, deprived of schooling, houses or opportunity, continued to suffer severe hardship.

Parliament reneged on the Treaty of Limerick, and the Penal Laws were enforced even more harshly. Dean Swift, Edmund Burke and others wrote scathingly of the plight of the poor, and the determination of the ascendancy to do nothing which might remove their own power and influence.

In the course of the eighteenth century, approximately one million people emigrated from Ireland to North America. These included Presbyterians from Ulster, who became the Scots-Irish pioneers of eighteenth-century American westward expansion. The example of the American War of Independence led members of the ascendancy in Ireland to seek some form of self-government for themselves, and in 1783 the Irish parliament in Dublin was granted a large measure of independence. Most of the Penal Laws were repealed.

THE UNITED IRISHMEN

The French Revolution, with its struggle for liberty, equality and fraternity, was regarded with great interest in Ireland, not least by Wolfe Tone, a Protestant lawyer. He sought to unite all Irish people, regardless of religion, in the struggle for an independent Irish parliament. The 'Society of United Irishmen' was an alliance of Irish Catholics and Ulster Protestants.

Their intention was to seek peaceful reform, but when the government denied emancipation to Catholics, they resorted to force. Wolfe Tone went to France for help. The French, who were at war with Britain, supplied 15,000 troops, but a severe storm prevented these reinforcements from landing.

The British were thoroughly alarmed, and the rebellion was savagely defeated with the loss of 30,000 lives. The United Irish leaders were executed. Wolfe Tone committed suicide in prison. He is revered as a great hero of Irish nationalism. The 1798 rising was one of the very few occasions when Presbyterians in Ulster joined southern Catholics in rebellion against the English crown, though it is perhaps more accurate to speak of two simultaneous rebellions, each confined to its own sectarian grouping – Presbyterians in Ulster, Catholics in Wexford.

From the British point of view, disaster had been averted, partly by good fortune, and pressure was brought to bear upon members of the Dublin parliament to disband themselves. This they did in 1801, when direct rule was imposed from London under the Act of Union. Ireland was now a part of the United Kingdom.

The remnants of the United Irish leaders attempted a further rising against British authority in Ireland in 1803, led by Robert Emmett: it failed. Another passionate hero of resistance, Emmett was arrested, and made a long and emotional confession of his political faith from the dock. He said he would not permit his epitaph to be written 'until my country takes its place among the nations.'

DANIEL O'CONNELL

In the nineteenth century, the gulf between the two communities widened. Attempts were made to secure Catholic emancipation, but without success. Daniel O'Connell, a lawyer from Kerry who had been educated in France, realized that the only hope lay in mass protest. He concentrated his energies on the rural Catholic people, and by 1823 formed the Catholic Association, whose membership subscription – a penny a month – was sufficiently low for almost anyone to join. O'Connell was thus able to accumulate the Catholic vote, and in 1826 his candidate (a Protestant, incidentally) defeated his 'establishment' opponent in an election in Clare by a huge margin.

O'Connell was elected to parliament three years later, though barred as a Catholic from taking his seat at Westminster. The increasing strength of Catholic influence led the Westminster parliament to give in and pass a Bill, for the first time emancipating Catholics, in 1829.

O'Connell, who had been much influenced by the violence of the French Revolution, was himself opposed to the use of force. However, he set his energies towards repealing the Act of Union and the reinstatement of the Irish parliament. He addressed enormous gatherings of people, but stopped short of violent confrontation, to the despair of many of his followers.

As the confidence of Catholic nationalists grew during the first half of the nineteenth century, the Presbyterians, who were largely in the north, saw their future as lying increasingly with the Establishment, paving the way for the emergence of a unionist political party. At the same time, the concept of 'Irishness' came more and more to be seen as synonymous with Roman Catholicism.

From the 1850s and 60s onward, the north east rapidly became industrialized, based on textiles, and machine goods and ship-building in Belfast. This increased the uneven development of North East Ireland in relation to the rest. It also resulted, in trading terms, in a maritime triangle based on the rivers Lagan, Mersey and Clyde. Naturally, it reinforced the Protestant sense of interest in maintaining the Union.

THE GREAT FAMINE

By 1840 the population of Ireland had reached eight million. The rural poor were dependent for food largely upon the potato. In 1845 a virulent form of blight destroyed a large part of the potato harvest in the south-east. The following year it spread through the country and by 1847 almost the entire crop was destroyed. The margin of subsistence was a very fine one, and a large part of the population was threatened with starvation.

The famine was not purely a natural disaster. Peasants produced sufficient food, but were obliged to sell it in order to pay rent to their landlords. Government officials appreciated that the system of agriculture and land tenure was much to blame for the hardship, and were angry and frustrated at the behaviour of many landlords. Throughout the famine years, ships laden with grain and cattle continued to leave Ireland daily for England.

The government was unprepared for such a crisis, and immense suffering had occurred before any system of relief could be devised. In 1847, however, the government was forced to provide direct assistance. It imported maize from India and America, which was used as 'payment' for special construction works, and set up soup kitchens. The construction projects included the 'famine roads' which often led nowhere, and petered out in the countryside. At the same time, *laissez-faire* economic policies allowed the market to run unchecked, and permitted uncontrolled speculation in food commodities.

Government policies changed frequently. There was no efficient local organization. Much relief depended on charity. The Poor Law Act of 1847 allowed relief outdoors as well as in the workhouses, but restricted such assistance to those who held less than a quarter-acre of ground, thus forcing many at the margins to give up their meagre land. An attempted rising by the 'Young Ireland' group, led by William Smith O'Brien, was headed off by the government and failed miserably.

By the end of 1851 nearly a million people had died, and more than the same number had emigrated, the majority to America, but also to Canada and Australia and to Britain. Thousands of the most destitute got no further than Liverpool.

Horrible as the famine was, and it remains etched into the Irish psyche as the prime example of British heartlessness towards the Irish people, the after-effects were no less devastating. The population of Ireland effectively halved to four and a half million by the end of the century, though it is arguable that many would have been forced to emigrate in any case. But the bitterness and anger which were carried overseas by those who left were to have lasting consequences. At home, smallholders were cleared from the land in large numbers, and the profits of landowners, many of them absentees, increased. Attempts by sympathetic MPs to secure fixed tenure and fair rents failed in parliament in 1852.

THE FENIANS

The newly-arrived Irish in America organized politically, and many influenced and financed affairs back home, with the intention of creating an Irish republic by force. The Fenians originated in New York. They spread throughout Ireland in the 1860s and became the Irish Republican Brotherhood, the precursors of the IRA. The Brotherhood was a secret society whose loyalty was to the republican cause. The IRB trained and equipped small groups in Britain and Ireland, but were unable to mount a concerted campaign. Instead, they mounted isolated attacks on military and police targets.

The Roman Catholic Church vehemently opposed the new movement, partly because it was a secret society, but also on account of the potential threat which it posed to the influence of the Church. Yet the Fenian movement was supported by many clergy, and most of its members were practising Catholics.

CHARLES STEWART PARNELL AND HOME RULE

Many of the Fenians became involved with the Irish Land League. This organization aimed to give land to the farmers who worked it, and to protect them against unjust rent increases and eviction. Landlords were to be ignored, or 'boycotted' – Captain Boycott was an early victim.

Charles Stewart Parnell, a Protestant Irish MP, became president of the Land League, which was remarkably successful. After a largely non-violent campaign, a series of Acts transferred more than half the land in Ireland from landlords to tenants, who were able to acquire small – often very small – holdings on fixed tenure and at fair rents. Protestants were prominently involved in the land campaign.

Parnell then turned his attention to the demand for Home Rule in Ireland – an Irish parliament to legislate for Irish affairs. In 1884 nearly all adult males in Britain and Ireland were given the vote. Irish nationalists thereafter regularly won more than eighty per cent of Irish seats.

By 1886 home rule appeared imminent. Irish MPs held a balance between Tories and Liberals, and when William Ewart Gladstone converted to the cause, change seemed certain. Gladstone seems genuinely to have believed in home rule as a fundamental right, and as a remedy. His first Bill proposed an Irish parliament, with powers similar to those in the white colonies of the empire. However, many Liberals and most Conservatives opposed it. Lord Randolph Churchill raised fears among the Orangemen in Ulster. The Bill was lost by thirty votes, and the Liberals were defeated in the subsequent election.

Parnell could do little to influence the Conservative administration, which now took on the name Unionist, and made continued British rule in Ireland a major plank of policy. Parnell himself was discredited. His downfall was assured when he was named in a divorce petition, his private life having been ruthlessly exposed to the public gaze. In spite of a campaign to oust him, in which the Church took a prominent part, Parnell refused to resign, and split his party. He died in 1891 at the age of forty-six, from illness and exhaustion. Many believed his death had been brought on by the campaign of vilification. He was buried near O'Connell, and is remembered as a great Irish patriot.

The Liberals fell short of an overall majority in parliament in 1892, and Gladstone secured the support of Irish Nationalists with the promise of a further Home Rule Bill. This was a more limited proposal, under which powers would be devolved, but Irish members would continue to sit in Westminster. No particular provision was made for Ulster. The Bill passed the Commons but failed in the Lords. The issue was then effectively shelved for ten years.

The last years of the nineteenth century saw the beginnings of the Gaelic Revival. This sought to preserve and restore the Irish language, and to promote popular awareness of the cultural heritage in the arts and literature. Initially this movement, which was largely Protestant-inspired, was led by such figures as Yeats, Synge and Douglas Hyde. Later, under the influence of Padraig Pearse and others, it became more politically involved, and devoted to the cause of Irish independence. The movement became fiercely anti-English, and encouraged all things Irish, including language, dress, music and poetry. The Gaelic Athletic Association promoted Irish sports. The Gaelic Revival had an important effect on education – the Christian Brothers' Schools in particular were virulently anti-English and anti-Protestant. They influenced a number of nationalist leaders.

THE 1916 RISING

In parliament, the Irish Party under John Redmond succeeded at last in passing a Home Rule Bill in 1912, which was delayed until 1914 by the House of Lords. Loyalists in Ulster were incensed, and the Ulster Volunteer Force was formed, under the leadership of Edward Carson, and given training in combat. Their task was to defend Ulster if home rule was implemented. A Solemn League and Covenant was signed by nearly 250,000 people in September 1912, decrying Home Rule as disastrous for Ulster's well-being, and pledging to defend UK citizenship 'by all means which may be found necessary'. In the event, home rule was deferred on account of the First World War, after which the government promised it would be introduced, with special arrangements being made for Ulster.

Many Irishmen joined the British army. Others formed a considerable armed organization at home, the more radical of whom planned a rising during the war − 'Burn everything British except their coal.'

Sinn Féin ('Ourselves Together') had been formed in 1908 on a policy of withdrawal of Irish MPs from Westminster, and an independent Irish parliament. Assurances of Conservative support for armed resistance to home rule, together with anti-Catholic slogans, provoked nationalists in the south. Even moderates joined with Sinn Féin.

The result of these alliances was The Irish Volunteers, whose leaders, including Padraig Pearse, along with the Irish Citizens' Army, led by the Socialist leader James Connolly, prepared a rising for Easter Sunday 1916. Money was raised in America, and Sir Roger Casement was despatched to seek arms from Germany. In April 1916 a shipment of German arms was intercepted, and Casement was captured. This meant that the insurrection which was intended to take place in other parts of the country was a non-starter, and Eoin MacNeill, leader of the Irish Volunteers, published an order countermanding the Easter rising.

However, Pearse, Connolly and others decided to go ahead a day late. On Easter Monday, 1,600 men seized key installations, and the proclamation of an Irish republic was read in the General Post Office in Dublin. The British were taken by surprise, but soon rallied. By Friday over 300 lives had been lost, and Pearse and the insurrectionists surrendered in front of the Post Office, which bears the scars of the conflict to this day.

That might perhaps have been the end of the matter, but for Britain's subsequent actions. Pearse, Connolly and the other five signatories of the proclamation, along with nine others, were shot, and over 2,000 taken prisoner. Casement was hanged for treason.

These executions caused widespread revulsion, and the leaders of the rising were hailed as heroes. Support for Sinn Féin soared. In 1918 Sinn Féin and Home Rule members were elected in a landslide. These refused to take up their Westminster seats, and set up an Irish parliament in Dublin. This parliament, called Dáil Éireann (Assembly of Ireland) proclaimed a Republic in January 1919, with Eamon de Valera as President.

During the First World War, the Ulster Volunteer Force had joined the British Army (as the '36th Division') and suffered enormous losses at the Battle of the Somme. Over 100,000 Roman Catholic Irish also joined.

IRELAND DIVIDED

The Dáil was not recognized by Britain, and indeed was proscribed in September 1919. Yet it continued to govern, establishing a system of local government and administration of justice and defence. The Irish Volunteers became the Irish Republican Army. A campaign of attacks on police and military targets was mounted by the IRA. In the north, Catholic workmen were attacked by unionists in Belfast, and a virtual state of civil war ensued.

The British reacted by drafting in what was in effect a paramilitary force, though described as auxiliary policemen. These became known as the 'Black and Tans', after their distinctive uniforms. The Black and Tans acquired a reputation for particular viciousness and provoked Michael Collins, a survivor of the 1916 rising, to lead a campaign of resistance which was scarcely less ruthless.

Neither side was able to win, but the British Prime Minister, Lloyd George, was sufficiently alarmed by the situation to impose a settlement in 1920. The Government of Ireland Act provided for two parliaments in Ireland. One was for Northern Ireland, which was to comprise six of the counties of Ulster, the other three being excluded to ensure a Protestant majority. The second parliament was to govern the remaining twenty-six counties, which were to be called Southern Ireland.

Both would also have representatives in the British parliament, and a Council of Ireland would be formed. The two parliaments had powers to federate or unite, but otherwise their activities were to be very limited.

This arrangement was quite unacceptable to Sinn Féin. It was supported, however, albeit reluctantly, by Ulster unionists. The following year, unionists won a sizeable majority in Northern Ireland, while republicans gained almost all seats in the South. A delegation from the Dáil went to London to negotiate.

They proposed a neutral, all-Ireland state. Lloyd George, having failed to coerce the northern unionists into an association with the south, determined that the loyalists were not to be forced into an all-Ireland state. A treaty was drawn up, establishing the 'Irish Free State' in the whole of Ireland, but permitting Northern Ireland to opt out and retain its separate status. The new state was to remain part of the British empire, and to retain allegiance to the British crown.

This tactic was an attempt to deal separately with the two Irish groups. Having dealt with the unionists in the 1920 Act, Lloyd George could treat with the Sinn Féiners in relation to the twenty-six counties.

CIVIL WAR

In spite of opposition from de Valera and others, this Treaty was narrowly passed in the Dáil in January 1922. De Valera resigned. The republican movement split. Sinn Féin boycotted what it saw as an illegal assembly in Dublin, and continued its campaign of violence in the North. The stage was set for the Irish Civil War.

This broke out in June 1922, between those who were prepared to support the treaty that gave independence to the south of Ireland, and those who rejected it. The war was fiercely fought on both sides. The IRA leader, Michael Collins, was assassinated. In 1923 the Dáil, boycotted by Sinn Féin, passed the constitution of the new Irish Free State. The IRA continued to fight for a united Irish republic.

THE IRISH FREE STATE

The supporters of the Treaty formed a party which came to be called Fine Gael (Irish Family). In 1926 de Valera formed Fianna Fáil (Soldiers of Ireland). The Free State Government, led by William Cosgrave, was beset by post civil-war domestic difficulties – continuing emigration, desperate poverty and severe shortage of housing.

The Roman Catholic Church exercised considerable influence in the life of the Free State. Divorce was prohibited, along with artificial means of contraception, and strict censorship of written material was enforced. The Church's involvement in education, which had developed along sectarian lines, became even stronger.

In 1937 de Valera, in power at the head of a Fianna Fáil government, drew up a new constitution which was established by referendum. It removed the oath of allegiance to the British crown, and incorporated 'Catholic Clauses', with special recognition for the Roman Catholic Church. Whilst it was implicitly a constitution to govern the twenty-six counties, Articles 2 and 3 laid claim to the whole island. In 1938 Douglas Hyde, a Protestant, became the first President of the Irish Republic.

THE NEW REPUBLIC

Eamon de Valera, as Prime Minister (Taoiseach) asserted Ireland's right to remain neutral in the 1939–45 war, in the face of strong pressure from both Churchill and President Roosevelt. In point of fact, many Irish people supported the fight against Nazism, and thousands served in the British forces. De Valera and his government, however, held that a state which saw itself as forcibly partitioned could not, without compromising its integrity, fight alongside Britain in defence of democracy. The effect of the war was to widen the gulf between the two traditions in Ireland.

In 1949 a coalition government declared that the state would henceforth be described as the Republic of Ireland. At the same time, Ireland left the Commonwealth.

Since 1949 the southern Republic ('Eire') has undergone

continuous political development. Along with Britain, it joined the European Community in 1972, and has benefited considerably from Regional Development Grants and the Social Fund. Suggestions that membership of the EC would initiate wider debate about the problems of the North have scarcely materialized, however, at least until the peace process developed towards the end of 1994.

NORTHERN IRELAND

The Ireland Act at Westminster stated that a change in the constitutional status of the North could only occur with the consent of the northern parliament. Northern Ireland had its own parliament for the six counties at Stormont, in Belfast, but it also returned MP's to Westminster. The Stormont government was under the permanent control of the Unionist Party; indeed, careful steps were taken to ensure that this would always be the case. There was never a chance for the minority nationalist parties to gain power, or even to share in it in a meaningful way.

The apparently secure position of the unionists was, in fact, an illusion. They felt deeply insecure. Hence the descendants of the Protestant settlers have always been defensive and, although they would describe themselves as British to the core, have often been in conflict with the parliament in Britain. They regarded Catholics as, at best, reluctant to accept the legitimacy of the state or to support it, while at the same time drawing benefits from it, especially in provision for education.

The issue of religion in the Northern conflict is a complex one. It is important to note that within the unionist community, there has always been a strong degree of fear and hatred of Roman Catholicism. Catholics were – and often are – regarded as disloyal by nature, and less than trustworthy. This fear was exacerbated by the rapid decline of the Protestant population in the South after 1920. Catholic reaction to Protestantism and its adherents has tended to be more political than religious.

Between 1956 and 1962 the IRA continued a sporadic campaign of violence, particularly along the border, with the continuing aim of securing a united Ireland, chiefly by wearing down resistance, and forcing Britain to leave.

In 1963 Terence O'Neill became Prime Minister of Northern Ireland, and brought in certain reforms, allowing Catholics better access to public housing and removing some of the more glaring prohibitions in employment. He also, for the first time, exchanged visits with the Taoiseach, Sean Lemass. O'Neill was attacked from within his own 'official' Unionist Party, especially by the Revd Ian Paisley, who formed the breakaway Democratic Unionist Party. O'Neill was forced out of office.

THE TROUBLES

In the late 1960s the Catholic community began to protest against the lack of civil rights within Northern Ireland. The Civil Rights Association was not concerned with a united Ireland. The Stormont government, however, viewed it as an attempt to undermine the Northern state.

Marches and demonstrations were held in 1968, many of them broken up by the police, and taunted by extreme Protestants. The following year there was serious rioting in Burntollet, Belfast and Londonderry (Derry), where the police first used plastic bullets to quell a civil disturbance in the Catholic Bogside area of the city.

The British army was drafted in, at the request of Stormont, with the intention of offering support to the Royal Ulster Constabulary, which had lost control of public order. Indeed, loyalist mobs were burning Catholics out of their homes in Belfast. The Labour government in Britain insisted on reforms. The armed Special Constabulary, known as the 'B specials', composed almost entirely of Protestant Orangemen, was disbanded. Public housing was entrusted to a non-political body and legislation against discrimination in employment was introduced. In 1970 a new political party was formed in the North, the Social and Democratic Labour Party (SDLP), in order to better organize the 'new' nationalists for participation in the political process.

The following year the first British soldier was killed by the 'Provisional' IRA, which had broken away from the official IRA the previous year. Internment without trial was introduced by Prime Minister Brian Faulkner, against the advice of senior army officers but with the agreement of the Westminster parliament. It had been used with some success in 1922, 1939 and 1956, but was now used only against republicans – on a very poorly devised police list, which included many who had no record of violent politics. This led to further widespread rioting, especially in Belfast, which worsened when it was reported that a number of internees had suffered ill-treatment while in captivity.

The year 1972 was a critical turning-point in the troubles. On 30 January, thirteen unarmed men were shot dead by the army in Derry on what became known as 'Bloody Sunday'. Horror at this act was not confined to the North: the British Embassy in Dublin was burnt down as a reprisal. The official enquiry into Bloody Sunday, conducted by Lord Chief Justice Widgery, exonerated the Parachute Regiment, and was regarded by nationalists as a deliberate 'whitewash', adding to their sense of outrage.

DIRECT RULE

In March 1972 the British Prime Minister, Edward Heath, announced the abolition of Stormont, and the assumption of direct rule of the province by Westminster, under a Secretary of State. This did nothing to diminish the violence. The Provisional IRA killed nine people and injured a hundred and thirty with bombs in Belfast on 'Bloody Friday', 21 July.

At the same time, Protestant paramilitary groups were gaining support, among them the Ulster Defence Association, Ulster Freedom Fighters and the Ulster Volunteer Force. Sectarian murders of Catholics began to exceed those of Protestants. In 1973, the British Government produced a White Paper with proposals for a power-sharing executive. Heath called a constitutional conference at Sunningdale, attended by representatives of the British and Irish Governments and of both communities in Northern Ireland. They discussed North–South relations and a Council of Ireland. All the representatives agreed that there could be no change in the constitutional status of Northern Ireland without the consent of the majority of its people.

The power-sharing Executive was established in 1974, consisting of unionists (in point of fact a minority of them who shared Faulkner's views), the SDLP and Alliance parties. The experiment was short-lived. A British general election in February 1974 was viewed in Northern Ireland as a referendum on the Executive, which was decisively rejected by unionist voters. It was brought down by a massive strike of Protestant workers, called by the Ulster Workers' Council and extreme unionists. The strike paralysed key services in the province. The newly-elected Labour Government of Harold Wilson would not risk using the army, which had advised that it lacked the technical capability to run essential services.

Loyalist terrorists carried violence into the Republic in 1974, with bombs in Dublin and County Monaghan, killing thirty civilians. Internment was phased out in 1975. Hopes of reconciliation were raised in 1976 with large demonstrations by the 'Peace People', but these proved to be only a short-lived response to the continuing violence.

In 1975, Secretary of State Merlyn Rees removed 'special category' status from loyalist and republican prisoners, and normalized prison conditions with those in other parts of the United Kingdom.

In 1978 Republican prisoners in the Maze Prison launched a 'dirty protest' in support of better conditions, and recognition of their status as political, rather than criminal, prisoners. In 1979 a Conservative Northern Ireland spokesman, Airey Neave, was killed by a car bomb within the Palace of Westminster by the Irish National Liberation Army. Earl Mountbatten, who spent a month each year in the Republic without protection, was killed in Sligo, and eighteen British soldiers were ambushed and killed at Warrenpoint on the same day.

In 1980 Margaret Thatcher and the Taoiseach, Charles Haughey, agreed on 'new and closer political co-operation'. Republican prisoners began a 'fast unto death' in support of their campaign for political status, but called it off. However, the following year a new hunger strike began. Bobby Sands was elected to the Westminster parliament for Sinn Féin (the first time the party had contested a Westminster seat) while in prison on hunger strike. Sands died on the sixty-sixth day of his fast. This was followed by a further nine deaths between May and August.

In 1982 Provisional Sinn Féin polled ten per cent of votes in elections for a Northern Ireland Assembly, but they and the SDLP refused to take their seats. Secretary of State Jim Prior's experiment in devolution of power on a 'rolling' basis was abandoned. Several prisoners stood in southern elections for the Dáil and two were elected. The Provisional IRA took its campaign of terrorist violence to Britain, exploding a car bomb outside Harrods store in London, which killed five people and injured eighty.

In 1984 the New Ireland Forum produced a report recommending unity by consent. It asserted the right of people in the North to a British cultural identity, while denying them the 'right' to live in the UK. It proposed three possible solutions to the constitutional position of the North: a Unitary State (the preferred option), a Federal Ireland, or Joint Authority. The reaction of Margaret Thatcher was to say 'Out, out, out,' though discussions continued between the two governments.

President Reagan, on a visit to the Republic to discover his Irish roots, called for an end to violence in Northern Ireland. At the Conservative Party conference in Brighton in November 1984 the Provisional IRA succeeded in bombing the conference hotel, narrowly missing the Prime Minister, and killing five people.

THE ANGLO-IRISH AGREEMENT

In 1985, largely through the constant efforts of the leader of the SDLP, John Hume, an Anglo-Irish agreement was signed by the British Prime Minister and the Taoiseach, Garret FitzGerald, 'to develop the unique relationship between [the] two peoples'. Under the terms of the agreement, the Dublin government was enabled to make representations on matters which affected the nationalist community in the North. Regular meetings were established and a permanent secretariat formed.

Unionists opposed the Agreement from the start, on the grounds that they had not been consulted, and the unacceptability of 'interference' in the affairs of Northern Ireland by a foreign power. In 1986 they resigned from the House of Commons *en masse,* forcing fifteen by-elections. They refused to co-operate in local government and held massive demonstrations. Loyalist paramilitary activity increased, including attacks on off-duty RUC personnel and their families.

In June 1987 Sinn Féin won nine per cent of the Northern Ireland vote in the UK general election. In November, a Provisional IRA bomb in Enniskillen killed eleven people attending a Remembrance Day service. This resulted in massive worldwide condemnation. In March 1988, three IRA 'activists' were shot by British security forces in Gibraltar. At their funerals, three mourners were killed by a loyalist gunman, and fifty others injured.

THE DOWNING STREET DECLARATION AND THE PEACE PROCESS

It would be possible to go on chronicling in minute detail the ceaseless succession of atrocity and counter-atrocity. It is sufficient to say that violence continued unabated until the autumn of 1994, though at an average of seventy-eight deaths a year compared with four hundred and fifty in 1972. It will be readily apparent that the roots of this violence, on both sides, lie in the troubled history of the island of Ireland and its peoples. Although constantly reported in the British media, there is an extraordinary degree of apathy in Britain, even in the wake of major terrorist attacks here, such as the Guildford bomb which killed four people, and the Birmingham bombs which killed nineteen, in 1974. There is also considerable ignorance even of the principal landmarks of Anglo-Irish, or more correctly British-Irish, history.

On 20 March 1993 a Provisional IRA bomb exploded in Warrington, near Liverpool, killing two children and injuring fifty-six people. There was widespread revulsion in Britain, and a demonstration by 20,000 people in Dublin, yet many in Northern Ireland reflected that their own daily experience of violence and death had received little comparable attention. The President of Ireland, Mary Robinson, attended a memorial service in Warrington, and President Clinton sent a message condemning violence 'from whatever quarter' and calling for dialogue. Prime Minister John Major declared that there was now an opportunity to 'catch the mood' and recommence talks between the British and Irish governments and the constitutional parties in the North.

In April 1993 John Hume met with Gerry Adams of Sinn Féin for talks in Derry – the first such face-to-face discussions for more than two years. In point of fact, Hume and Adams had met as long ago as 1988. Much of the approach taken by Peter Brooke and Sir Patrick Mayhew, successive Secretaries of State, and in the Downing Street Declaration of December 1993, was a response to the issues raised then. Mayhew, speaking in Liverpool, expressed the government's wish to return 'wide powers and responsibilities' to locally-elected politicians. A very large bomb devastated part of the financial centre of the City of London in April, causing £1 billion of damage.

Towards the end of 1993 it was revealed that secret 'indirect' contacts had been taking place between British officials and Sinn Féin, though it had previously been strenuously denied that contacts existed. In December John Major and Taoiseach Albert Reynolds announced a new framework for constitutional arrangements.

The Irish government acknowledged the right of Northern Ireland to determine its own future. Dublin has also suggested that the Republic's claim to the whole island (Articles 2 and 3) might be negotiable in the context of an overall settlement. The British government stated that it has no strategic military or economic interest in Northern Ireland.

In December 1993 the two leaders issued the 'Downing Street Declaration'. John Major declared on television that it was time for the people of Ireland to 'put the poison of history behind them'. The agreement cleared the way for all-party talks, which could include Sinn Féin if they ceased violence. It opened the possibility of parallel referenda on the border, North and South, and stated that a united Ireland would not be resisted if achieved by peaceful means. Ian Paisley, before he had read the document, said to Major, 'You have sold Ulster to buy off the fiendish republican scum.'

By the end of 1994 there was a mood in Northern Ireland of relief and enjoyment of a new-found absence of conflict, but probably more uncertainty about who was going to pay the price of change than real optimism.

A NEW FRAMEWORK FOR AGREEMENT

In February 1995 two documents were published for discussion. The first – 'A Framework for Accountable Government in Northern Ireland' – was issued by the British Government. It proposed a single-chamber assembly of about ninety members, having executive and legislative responsibilities over as wide a range of subjects as the old Northern Ireland parliament had, and a system of checks and balances to give reassurance to 'both main sections' of the community.

The second document – 'A New Framework for Agreement' – came from both the British and Irish governments. It reaffirmed principles of self-determination and consent, and protection for 'the rights and identities of both traditions'. Each government proposed changes in its constitutional legislation – in the British case, to incorporate a willingness to accept the will of a majority of the people living in Northern Ireland for any change, and to exercise jurisdiction with 'rigorous impartiality'. The Irish government would propose changes in the Irish Constitution, to remove any territorial claim to jurisdiction over Northern Ireland.

A new North/South body was proposed, to deal with matters of mutual concern, accountable to a Northern Ireland Assembly and the Irish parliament. The document envisaged more extensive co-operation between the British and Irish governments, and a new Intergovernmental Conference. The key to any change in the constitutional status of Northern Ireland was to be 'agreement by the parties, and then by the people'.

It seems likely that all-party talks (or at least all willing parties) will be held, and that paramilitaries of both traditions, having forsworn violence, will be permitted to express their views, notwithstanding the arsenal of weapons still presumably held by both sides.

Writing in August 1995, it remains to be seen whether the unhealed wounds of eight centuries will form the heart of the agenda. If so, there may be grounds for optimism as well as hope. If not, the present euphoria may turn again to yet further grief.

Appendix Two
Reconciliation projects in Britain and Ireland

There are many projects in Northern Ireland and the Republic, concerned to promote peace, reconciliation and community relations. I have listed only a few of the better-known ones. A comprehensive 'Guide to Peace, Reconciliation and Community Relations Projects in Ireland' compiled by Joe Hinds, is available from:

Community Relations Council
6 Murray Street
Belfast BT1 6DN

It may also be ordered through book shops:
ISBN 1 898 273-03-X.

BRITISH IRISH ASSOCIATION
154 Buckingham Palace Road
London SW1W 9TR

An independent organization to promote better relations between the communities in both islands. Organizes regular conferences.

BRITISH IRISH EXCHANGE
c/o 14 Hogarth Avenue
Reading
Berkshire RG3 2HD

Facilitates exchanges between like-minded people from all parts of Ireland and Britain.

CHRISTIAN RENEWAL CENTRE
Shore Road
Rostrevor
Co Down BT34 3ET

An established community of Protestant and Catholic Christians praying and working together for reconciliation. The Centre is a place of prayer, renewal and reconciliation. A regular prayer letter/bulletin is published.

THE CORRYMEELA COMMUNITY
Corrymeela Centre
Ballycastle
Co Antrim BT54 6QU

A dispersed community of Protestant and Catholic Christians committed to work for reconciliation wherever they live and work. There are two centres in Ballycastle and Belfast, and local cell groups in Northern Ireland, the Republic and Britain.

FELLOWSHIP OF RECONCILIATION (NI)
Reconciliation Ireland
224 Lisburn Road
Belfast BT9 6GB

As its name implies, its faith and motives have for many years been directed towards disarmament, mediation, active non-violence and the removal of injustices. FOR(NI) seeks to devise and apply non-violent methods of resolving conflict and changing society. FOR(NI) is a member of the International Fellowship of Reconciliation, which publishes a newsletter in Britain and Northern Ireland.

GLENCREE CENTRE FOR RECONCILIATION
37 Upper Fitzwilliam Street
Dublin 2
Republic of Ireland

Aims to promote good relationships between the Republic and its neighbours, especially in Northern Ireland, Great Britain and the European Union. Has a Peace and Reconciliation Centre in Co Wicklow.

IRISH SCHOOL OF ECUMENICS
Milltown Park
Sandford Road
Dublin 6
Republic of Ireland

An international academic institute, Christian and interdenominational. Promotes the unity of Christians through teaching, research and extra-mural activities. Promotes dialogue between religions, and work for peace and justice in Ireland and abroad. Various courses of adult education and post-graduate courses.

NATIONAL PEACE COUNCIL
88 Islington High Street
London N1 8EG

An independent umbrella organization which co-ordinates the activities of groups involved in all aspects of peace work. A Northern Ireland working group aims to inform people in Britain about the background to the conflict in Ireland, and to suggest possible actions for peace.

Notes

CHAPTER ONE
1. David Sheppard and Derek Worlock, *Better Together* (London, Hodder & Stoughton, 1988).
2. David Sheppard and Derek Worlock, *With Hope in our Hearts* (London, Hodder & Stoughton, 1994).

CHAPTER TWO
1. John Austin Baker, 'Ireland and Northern Ireland' in *The Challenge of Northern Ireland* (Maynooth, The Furrow Trust, 1984).

CHAPTER THREE
1. Morgan Llewellyn, letter in the *Independent,* 7 April 1993.

CHAPTER FOUR
1. Donald Bird, letter in the *Church Times,* 7 May 1993.
2. Maya Angelou, *On the Pulse of Morning,* Poem for the Inauguration of the President of the United States of America (New York, Random House, 1993; London, Virago, 1993).
3. Conference promoted by Hope in the Cities (MRA) and the City of Richmond, Va., June 1993.
4. Hugh Montefiore, the closing words of a sermon 'The other sex' in *Truth to Tell: A Radical Restatement of the Christian Faith* (London, Fontana, 1966).

CHAPTER FIVE
1. Mary Robinson, speech at a conference to launch the Warrington Project, 9 October 1993.
2. Stephen Kingsnorth, letter to the *Irish Times,* 13 May 1993.
3. Robin Eames, *Chains to be Broken* (Belfast, Blackstaff Press, 1993): a helpful introduction to the roots and consequences of sectarian division in Northern Ireland.
4. George Carey, sermon in Christ Church Cathedral, Dublin, 18 November 1994.

CHAPTER SIX
1. Henry Manning, letter to Earl Grey, 1868.
2. Don Simpson, *Cardinal Manning in Ireland* (unpublished paper).

3. Patrick Mayhew, 'Culture and Identity', speech given in Coleraine, 16 December 1992.
4. Letter to the *Independent*, c.9 March 1994.
5. Alec Porter, unpublished paper.
6. Mitchel Mclaughlin, 'Protestantism, Unionism and Loyalism', in *Fingerpost* (a Derry community magazine).

CHAPTER SEVEN

1. In this chapter, extensive use is made of quotations from *Nothing but the Same Old Story: The Roots of Anti-Irish Racism* (Information on Ireland, 1984) by kind permission of the author, Liz Curtis.
2. Colin O'Brien Winter, sermon preached in St John's Church, Peckham on the Feast of St John Chrysostom, 1974. John Chrysostom was also a bishop in exile.
3. Giraldus Cambrensis (Gerald of Wales), *The History and Topography of Ireland* (London, Penguin Classics, 1985).
4. Edmund Spenser, *A View of the State of Ireland* (1596), quoted by Ned Lebow, *Eire – Ireland*, vol. VIII, no. 4, Winter 1973.
5. Quoted Lebow, op. cit.
6. David Hume, *History of England* (1750s), quoted by Lebow, op. cit.
7. Jonathan Swift, *Gulliver's Travels* (1726) (Everyman Library edn, 1991).
8. John Curry, 1775, quoted by Lebow, op. cit.
9. Arthur Young, *A Tour in Ireland* (1770), quoted by Stephen J. Campbell, *The Great Irish Famine* (Strokestown, The Famine Museum, 1994).
10. Arthur Young, op. cit., quoted by Mary Campbell on BBC Radio 4, 29 December 1983 in a documentary, 'Paddy in his wellies'.
11. *Punch* 1848, quoted by Lebow, op. cit.
12. Sir Basil Brooke (1933), quoted by Michael Farrell, *Northern Ireland, The Orange State* (London, Pluto Press, 1980).
13. Brian Faulkner, speech. Date and circumstances unknown to the author.
14. Ian Paisley in the *Protestant Telegraph* (1967), quoted by Geoffrey Bell in *The Protestants of Ulster* (London, Pluto Press, 1976).
15. Loyalist song after Bloody Sunday 1972, quoted by Geoffrey Bell, op. cit.
16. Sydney Smith *Letters to Peter Plymley (The Works of the Reverend Sydney Smith)* (1807) (Longman, Brown, Green and Longmans, 1850).

CHAPTER EIGHT

1. Sunningdale Conference, December 1973 – the first conference since 1925 in which heads of government from Britain and both parts of Ireland participated.

2. Gordon Wilson, Submission to the Forum for Peace and Reconciliation, January 1995.

CHAPTER NINE

1. 'Bloody Sunday' is the name given to the killing of thirteen unarmed men in Derry by members of the Parachute Regiment on 30 January 1972. This, together with the subsequent Widgery Tribunal, is a continuing source of resentment in republican circles.

CHAPTER TEN

1. I am indebted for much of the background to this chapter to Robin Boyd: *Ireland – Christianity Discredited or Pilgrim's Progress?* (Geneva, WCC Publications, 1988), and to Norman Richardson, 'Understanding religion in Northern Ireland', a paper given at the launch of the Warrington Project, 9 October 1993.
2. Douglas Johnston and Cynthia Sampson, *Religion, the Missing Dimension of Statecraft* (Oxford, Centre for Strategic and International Studies and Oxford University Press, 1994).
3. See Appendix 2 for a list of reconciliation projects.
4. Johnston and Sampson, op. cit.
5. Terence McCaughey, *Memory and Redemption: Church, Politics and Prophetic Theology in Ireland* (Dublin, Gill & Macmillan, 1993).

CHAPTER ELEVEN

1. There are numerous references to evil in the Book of Psalms, among them, Pss. 34; 37; 40; 109; 140.
2. Albert Speer, quoted by Robert Elsberg, 'Truth Makes Demands on us', in *The Living Pulpit* (USA), vol. 1, no. 4.
3. Barbara Brown Taylor, 'The Evils of Pride and Self-Righteousness', in *The Living Pulpit,* vol. 1, no. 4.
4. John Austin Baker, 'Ireland and Northern Ireland' in *The Challenge of Northern Ireland* (Maynooth, The Furrow Trust, 1984).
5. I have drawn upon unpublished sermons of Douglas Powell with his permission, and upon a long discussion with him on the subject of penitence and penance, six months before his death.
6. The Prayer of Consecration in The Communion, Book of Common Prayer, 1662.
7. Richard von Weizsäcker, speech to the *Bundestag* of the Federal Republic of Germany, 8 May 1985, quoted by Donald W. Shriver Jr, *An Ethic for Enemies: Forgiveness in Politics* (Oxford, Oxford University Press, 1995).
8. Gareth Steadman Jones, 'When sorry is the right word', the *Independent,* 3 July 1995.
9. Donald W. Shriver, op. cit.

10. Gerald R. Ford, 'The American Promise', speech given on 19 February 1976, quoted by Shriver, op. cit.
11. George Bush, letter sent in October 1990, with compensation cheques, to Japanese-American former internees, quoted by Shriver, op. cit.
12. F. W. de Klerk, Nobel Laureate Lecture, Royal Albert Hall, London, 20 May 1994.
13. F. W. de Klerk, at a ceremony to unveil the flag of the 'new' South Africa, 29 April 1993.

CHAPTER TWELVE

1. Joint Declaration by the Prime Minister and the Taoiseach, 15 December 1993.
2. David Bleakley, *Peace in Ireland: Two States, One People* (London, Mowbray, 1995).
3. John Major, in an article in the *Belfast Telegraph* 1994, date unknown to the author.
4. Patrick Mayhew, 'Culture and Identity', speech in Coleraine, 16 December 1992.
5. John Whale, 'Thought for the Day', BBC Radio 4, on 1, 2 and 3 July 1980.
6. Denis Faul, interviewed on 'Newsnight', BBC 2, 1994, date unknown to the author.
7. Robert Southwell (1699), quoted by Terence Brown, *The Whole Protestant Community: The Making of a Historical Myth* (Field Day Pamphlet, Derry, 1985).
8. Kevin O'Higgins, speech in the Dáil, December 1925, quoted by Robert Kee, *Ireland, a History* (London, Weidenfeld and Nicholson, 1980).
9. Charles Stewart Parnell, speech in the House of Commons, 7 June 1886, quoted by T. W. Moody and F. X. Martin, *The Course of Irish History* (Radio Telefis Éireann and Mercier Press 1967 and 1984).
10. Terence Brown, *The Whole Protestant Community*, op. cit.
11. Jackie Redpath, article in the *Guardian*, 1 December 1993.
12. Timothy Kinahan, *Where do we go from here? Protestants and the Future of Northern Ireland* (Dublin, Columba Press, 1995).
13. John Austin Baker, 'Ireland and Northern Ireland' in *The Challenge of Northern Ireland* (Maynooth, The Furrow Trust, 1984).
14. Nelson Mandela, speaking on a visit to Dublin in 1990, quoted in the *New Internationalist*, May 1994.
15. Joan Tapsfield, 'An English Pilgrim in Northern Ireland 1977–1992', talk given at the Tirley Garth Conference Centre, Cheshire, 21 November 1992, published by Ivan and Maisie Poulton, 28 Lammas Road, London W5 5JB.
16. Joan Tapsfield in conversation with the author, June 1994.

17. Alan D. Falconer, 'The Road Leads On', paper given at the Annual Meeting of the Irish Council of Churches, 19 March 1994. See also Falconer (ed.) *Reconciling Memories* (Dublin, Columba Press, 1988).
18. Lord Hylton of Ammerdown, letter to Margaret Thatcher, 12 May 1981, reproduced by the Forgiveness and Politics Study Project, 2 Eaton Gate, London SW1.
19. Desmond Tutu, from the foreword to Brian Frost, *The Politics of Peace* (London, Darton, Longman & Todd, 1991).
20. Brian Frost, talk given to the Heswall Council of Churches, March 1994.
21. Brian Frost, *The Politics of Peace*.
22. Chris Brazier, 'The Fire and the Future' in *New Internationalist,* May 1994.
23. Naim Stifan Ateek, *Justice and Only Justice* (Maryknoll, Orbis Books, 1989).

CHAPTER THIRTEEN
1. Maya Angelou, *On the Pulse of Morning,* Poem for the Inauguration of the President of the United States of America (New York, Random House, 1993; London, Virago, 1993).
2. See Alan D. Falconer (ed.), *Reconciling Memories* (Dublin, Columba Press, 1988).
3. Martin Marty, 'Conflict and Conflict Resolution', in *The Living Pulpit* (USA), vol. 3, no. 3.
4. Daniel Corkery, *The Hidden Ireland: A Study of Gaelic Munster in the 18th Century* (first published 1924, Dublin, Gill & Macmillan, 1989).
5. Susan W. N. Ruach, 'A New Way of Struggling' in *The Living Pulpit* (USA) vol. 3, no. 3. Reproduced by kind permission of Susan W. N. Ruach and *The Living Pulpit*.

Further reading

This is a very select bibliography. I have arranged books which may be useful under different categories; naturally there is some overlap between them.

FORGIVENESS AND POLITICS
Ateek, Naim Stifan, *Justice and Only Justice* (Orbis Books).
Frost, Brian, *The Politics of Peace* (Darton, Longman & Todd).
Johnston, Douglas and Sampson, Cynthia (eds.), *Religion, the Missing Dimension of Statecraft* (Oxford University Press).
McCaughey, Terence P., *Memory and Redemption* (Gill & Macmillan).
Shriver, Donald W. Jr, *An Ethic for Enemies* (Oxford University Press).

THE GREAT FAMINE AND ITS CONSEQUENCES
Campbell, Stephen J., *The Great Irish Famine – Words and Images from the Famine Museum* (The Famine Museum, Strokestown Co., Roscommon, Republic of Ireland).
Kinealy, Christine, *This Great Calamity* (Gill & Macmillan).
Percival, John, *The Great Famine – Ireland's Potato Famine 1845–51* (BBC).
Scally, Robert James, *The End of Hidden Ireland – Rebellion, Famine and Emigration* (Oxford University Press).
Woodam Smith, Cecil, *The Great Hunger* (Hamish Hamilton).

HISTORY
Bew, Paul and Gillespie, Gordon, *Northern Ireland – A Chronology of the Troubles 1968–1993* (Gill & Macmillan).
Corkery, Daniel, *The Hidden Ireland – A Story of Gaelic Munster in the 18th Century* (Gill & Macmillan).
Foster, Roy P., *Modern Ireland 1600–1972* (Allen Lane and Penguin Books).
Kee, Robert, *Ireland – A History* (Weidenfeld & Nicholson, also Abacus paperback).
Moody, T. W. and Martin, F. X. (eds.), *The Course of Irish History* (RTE and Mercier Press).

THE RELIGIOUS DIMENSION
Boyd, Robin, *Ireland – Christianity Discredited or Pilgrim's Progress?* (World Council of Churches Publications, Geneva).

Carothers, J. Edward, *The Paralysis of Mainstream Protestant Leadership* (Abingdon Press, Nashville). [Refers to the United States, but is very useful.]

Dunlop, John, *A Precarious Belonging – Presbyterians and the Conflict in Ireland* (Blackstaff Press).

Eames, Robin, *Chains to be Broken* (Blackstaff Press).

Falconer, Alan D. (ed.), *Reconciling Memories* (Columba Press).

Galliher, John F. and Degregory, Jerry L., *Violence in Ireland – Understanding Protestant Perspectives* (Gill & Macmillan).

Interchurch Group on Faith and Politics, *Breaking down the Enmity – Faith and Politics in the Northern Ireland Conflict.*

Kinahan, Tim, *Where do we go from here? Protestants and the Future of Northern Ireland* (Columba Press).

Lee, Simon (ed.), *Freedom from fear – Churches together in Northern Ireland* (Institute of Irish Studies, Queens University of Belfast).

Lennon, Brian, SJ, *After the Ceasefires – Catholics and the Future of Northern Ireland* (Columba Press).

McVeigh, Joseph, *A Wounded Church – Religion, Politics and Justice in Ireland* (Mercier Press).

Sheppard, David and Worlock, Derek, *Better Together* (Hodder & Stoughton).

Sheppard, David and Worlock, Derek, *With Hope in Our Hearts* (Hodder & Stoughton).

PARTICULAR ISSUES

Bleakley, David, *Peace in Ireland – Two States, One People* (Mowbray). [Includes full texts of the Anglo-Irish Agreement 1985; the Downing Street declaration 1993; and Frameworks for the Future (a summary) 1995.]

Curtis, Liz, *Nothing but the same old story – the roots of anti-Irish racism* (Information on Ireland).

Hussey, Gemma, *Ireland Today – Anatomy of a Changing State* (Townhouse Viking).

McClean, Raymond, *The Road to Bloody Sunday* (Ward River Press).

McGarry, John and O'Leary, Brendan, *Time for Peace – Explaining Northern Ireland* (Blackwell).

O'Brien, Jack, *The Union-Jacking of Ireland* (Mercier Press).

Ryan, Mark, *War and Peace in Ireland – Britain and the IRA in the new world order* (Pluto Press).

Frameworks for the Future (HMSO 1995). [The 'Framework Documents'].

Parker, Michael (ed.), *The Hurt World – Short Stories of The Troubles* (Blackstaff Press). [We might learn more about the spirit and the achievements of the people of Northern Ireland over the past 25 years from this collection than from many of the more learned volumes listed above.]

The Society for Promoting Christian Knowledge (SPCK) has as its purpose three main tasks:

- Communicating the Christian faith in its rich diversity
- Helping people to understand the Christian faith and to develop their personal faith
- Equipping Christians for mission and ministry

SPCK Worldwide runs a substantial grant programme to support Christian literature and communication projects in over 100 countries. Special schemes also provide books for those training for ministry in many parts of the world. All gifts to SPCK are spent wholly on these grant programmes, without deductions.

SPCK Bookshops support the life of the Christian community by making available a full range of Christian literature and other resources, and by providing support to bookstalls and book agents throughout the UK. SPCK Bookshops' mail order department meets the needs of overseas customers and those unable to have access to local bookshops.

SPCK Publishing produces Christian books and resources, covering a wide range of inspirational, pastoral, practical and academic subjects. Authors are drawn from many different Christian traditions, and publications aim to meet the needs of a wide variety of readers in the UK and throughout the world.

The Society does not necessarily endorse the individual views contained in its publications, but hopes they stimulate readers to think about and further develop their Christian faith.

For further information about the Society, please write to:
SPCK, Holy Trinity Church, Marylebone Road,
London NW1 4DU, United Kingdom.
Telephone: 0171 387 5282